HENRY FONDA
and The Deputy

The Film and Stage Star
and His TV Western

Glenn A. Mosley

Dedication

To Sheri
and
my parents
of course

Henry Fonda and The Deputy—The Film and Stage Star and His TV Western
© 2011 Glenn A. Mosley. All rights reserved.

Published in the USA by:
BearManor Media
P O Box 71426
Albany, Georgia 31708
www.bearmanormedia.com

Printed in the United States of America
ISBN 978-1-59393-613-6

Book and cover design by Darlene Swanson • www.van-garde.com

Allen Case as Clay McCord and Henry Fonda
as Simon Fry in *The Deputy*. (Western TV Photos)

Contents:

Acknowledgements

In 1974, an anniversary retrospective of the landmark CBS television series *All in the Family* began with a famous actor saying, "Good Evening, I'm Henry Fonda." As a twelve-year-old boy in Massachusetts, I knew precisely who Henry Fonda was because this was back when local television stations did useful things such as making classic Hollywood films a regular—even daily-- part of their broadcast schedules. I first tip my hat, then, to the program schedulers at those old television stations in Boston, WSBK- TV and WKBG- TV; thanks for exposing me to the great Fonda films.

No writer with pets at home ever really writes alone. My cats Libby and Sallie were at my feet, and on the desk, respectively. Lady, the family dog, took long walks with me throughout Moscow, ID, at odd hours of the day and night, while I thought about this book.

Not enough can be said about the staff at the Interlibrary Loan Office at the University of Idaho Library in Moscow, and all those institutions who participate in ILL. I am also grateful to the staffs at UC- Santa Barbara, Davidson Library Special Collections, and Washington State University in Pullman, WA.

Able contributions also came from Jeff Kimberling, Roger L. Brown, Jay Mosley, Cam Mosley, Denise Bennett, Kathy Garver, Warren Berlinger, and Amanda Case, all of whom helped with either information gathering or technology needs. Special thanks to Norman Lear and Read Morgan for being so gracious with their time. Thanks also to Dr. Ron Evans at e/p partners TV for his supply of episodes.

The book could not have been completed without the superb technical and creative skills of Mary Katherine Packer. Mary, you are family.

My love and thanks to my lovely wife Sheri, who was patient not only with chatter about an old television series but also with the sound of Jack Marshall's theme and the refrain of Henry Fonda's voice emanating from the television.

My love and thanks to my mom and dad, the inestimable Carol and Carl Mosley. Not only did they allow me to buy my first television set, but they also knew the value of shutting it off.

Foreword

I was cast in *The Deputy* in 1960 when Henry Fonda saw my screen test and liked it. That's how I became Sergeant Tasker in the second season of the show; it was as simple as that. I was coming on as a regular after there had been several cast changes during the series' first year on the air.

Before we started shooting, I spoke with the producer, Mike Kraike, and asked him what kind of a guy Fonda was. "Don't go to him, let him come to you," he told me.

I followed Mike's advice; he knew Fonda better than I did. It turned out to be good advice.

Hank and I didn't speak the first two shows. At the beginning of the third show, on Monday morning, I came in, and he said, "Good morning, Read," and I said, "Good morning, Hank." He said, "Did you have a nice weekend?" "Beautiful," I said, and after that we were fine.

After the series was over—Fonda decided to end it himself-- I ran into him several months later at the Paramount lot in Hollywood. "Geez, Hank, have you any idea of the amount of money you cost me?" I said to him. He laughed and said, "Are you still in the business?"

Fonda was not a particularly outgoing guy, but once he liked you, you were in.

I enjoyed working with Henry Fonda and Allen Case on the series, and I know you'll enjoy Glenn Mosley's book about our days on *The Deputy*.

—Read Morgan

Prologue
LIFE ON THE SET OF TV WESTERNS, 1959- 1960

Approaching the summer of 1959, I decided I needed summer employment that paid me more than the $120 that I earned as a camp counselor on Catalina Island the two previous summers. That wasn't my weekly salary; that was $120 for each summer!

My uncle Harold was in charge of the set construction and studio operations at Republic Studios. With his help, I was able get a position on the "labor gang"; paying about $1.50 an hour, and time and a half for "overtime." That was a fortune to me at the time.

I would arrive at the "lot," and punch the time clock at 6am, and if there was no overtime, I would punch out at 2:30pm. That would give me enough time to hit the beach; however, that didn't happen often, as there always seemed to be more work to finish. We would move the various set and wall units from the stages and western street to the "scene dock" for storage, to be used again in another episode-- early recycling.

We would also dig holes for corrals, special effects, and stunts. The stuntmen would need a soft area to land, when they fell off a roof into the street; or when they were galloping away, and got "shot," and had to fall with the horse (the "falling horses" were trained to fall when they got the correct "cue" from the stuntman). The landing area would be selected by the director, and stuntman, depending on the staged action. We would then dig up the western street road base with a back hoe, or by hand, fill it with sand, and then add a thin layer of dirt on top, to blend in with the surrounding road. We would often standby to redo the surface for additional takes, and while waiting, we would wager on whether the stuntman, or his horse, would hit the "soft spot." More often than not, the horse would hit the sand, and the stuntman would bounce off the harder surface.

It was always a treat to report in, and find out that you were assigned to a "shooting company" for the day. At that time, most of the shows shot at Republic were westerns; *Wanted: Dead or Alive, The Rifleman, Gunsmoke, Zane Grey Theater,* etc. At the studio, there was a complete exterior western street; plus a western street inside, on two stages, for *Gunsmoke.* Shooting companies would also travel to various locations around Los Angeles: Vasquez Rocks, Bell Canyon Movie Ranch, Canejo, etc. These locations provided dirt roads, lakes, rock outcroppings, mine shafts, ranches, homesteads other western streets, etc. When you were with a shooting company, you were an "extra hammer"; you did whatever was requested, often helping the grips with erecting, or striking a set. Sometimes you would assist special effects with digging holes for explosions, and the like. Perhaps the most important detail we were required to attend to was the horse manure. Especially before a take, the assistant director would call for a "nine iron," and out I'd trot, with my trusty shovel, behind the offending horse, and remove the steaming mess.

Episodic television production in those days meant long days and hard work. The people who wrote, produced, and directed those programs—including my father, Christian Nyby, who directed episodes of many TV Westerns in those years—were dedicated professionals. That was true of the shows I worked on, and true of other shows, like *The Deputy*, as well.

Now that I am retired, after a long career as a TV film director, I find myself, in the morning, out in the barn, mucking out our horses stalls. I guess my life has now gone full circle.

— Christian I. Nyby II

Christian I. Nyby II directed hundreds of hours of episodic television during his long and successful career, which started on the set of television westerns in 1959. He was nominated for a Director's Guild Award in 1984 and received the Silver & Gold Award from the University of Idaho in 2010.

CHAPTER ONE

Fonda? On TV?

In 1959, *Newsweek* magazine quite understandably wondered out loud "Why an actor of Henry Fonda's distinction would strap on a pair of six guns next season and go loping around the screen as Marshal Simon Fry of the Southwest Arizona Territory."[1]

The television series in question was *The Deputy*, a television western series set to premiere in September 1959, over the NBC-TV network. The story of a marshal and his relationship with a local family in Silver City, Arizona, as he tried to maintain law and order, the series would star Fonda as Marshal Simon Fry, and co-star newcomer Allen Case (as local storekeeper and reluctant deputy Clay McCord), along with Hollywood veteran Wallace Ford (as Silver City Sheriff Herk Lamson), and young actress Betty Lou Keim (as Fran McCord, the sister of Clay McCord).

"But *Fonda?*" people asked. "On a TV show?"

This, after all, was *the* Henry Fonda— 54 years old, thirty years in show business and one of the most respected and popular stage and screen actors of the 20th century. His screen portrayals included

Mister Roberts, Tom Joad, Abraham Lincoln, and Wyatt Earp. On stage, he had known success in *Mister Roberts, The Caine Mutiny Court-Martial,* and *Point of No Return.* He was admired by his peers for his devotion to his craft. His standing with the American public was absolute—he stood for honesty and integrity.

And this was, after all, television. Not the generally well-regarded "Golden Age of Television" kind of television—anthology dramas— but *series* television, the sausage grinder infamous among actors and writers for the long hours, tough production schedules, and lack of time to do real creative work. Some even suggested that to work in series television was to essentially turn out the same product, week after week, with nothing to distinguish one episode from the next. "Many of my friends," Fonda wrote, "have asked why I've picked this season to debut in my own western series." [2]

Fonda, charismatic and honest as ever, said that the answer was "gold." "Gold convinced me," he said. "Residuals is a magic word. It means it rains gold. It is the only chance an actor has to save money these days."[3]

Fonda made no apologies for signing on the dotted line and committing to a television western series. The taming of the west, he told interviewers, was part of the national heritage and besides—"the thought of having an annuity from the residuals is very satisfying."[4]

The signing of Henry Fonda to a television series contract was big news in television in 1959. Fonda was, then and now, one of America's best and most beloved actors, and he brought enormous prestige to any project he was involved in. That he chose to give some of that prestige to a weekly television series surprised some, but sign on he did, and on September 12, 1959, Henry Fonda and *The Deputy* premiered on NBC- TV.

Henry Fonda as Simon Fry in *The Deputy*.
(*c.* 1978 Tom Kelley/mptvimages.com)

While never a hit, the series started off to serviceable ratings and then cooled off, only to regain some footing as the first season came to a close. Much of the problem with the ratings was directly traceable to the fact that when Fonda agreed to star in the series, his agents arranged it so that he only had the lead in six of the season's thirty-nine episodes, while appearing just briefly in all the rest.

Fonda called this having his cake and eating it, too—being able to fulfill his responsibilities to *The Deputy* in a twelve-week time frame and leaving the rest of the year open for other work, be it in film or on the stage. *Newsweek* described this, somewhat cynically, as allowing Fonda to work on the series and "then devote himself to more serious concerns."[5] (Among the other work Fonda did during the production of *The Deputy* were the plays *Silent Night, Lonely Night* and *Critic's Choice*.)

But Fonda would not have agreed to do the series at all unless that deal was in place. When approached about the possibility of signing on for the series, Fonda rejected the idea at first. "I told my agents," he said, "'after all, fellows, is there really room for another western?' They laughed at me and came up with agency and Madison Avenue figures. I don't know if they know what they're talking about, but I wanted to get in before it was too late."[6]

Fonda's initial reluctance really didn't have anything to do with a dislike for the western genre with which he was so closely identified, somewhat to his chagrin (the taxi drivers, he said, were always asking him when he was going to do another western). He said westerns were fine—"If they're good, with believable characters and some humor and credible situations, instead of 'they went thataway' incidents."[7] What Fonda had been concerned with was becoming closely identified as a single character.

Marshal Fry mentors his reluctant deputy,
Clay McCord. (Personality Photos)

Truth was, the television western was peaking as a popular genre in 1959, and Fonda got in with *The Deputy* just before the end. The series ran for 76 episodes over two seasons, and would have run for at least one more had Fonda not pulled the plug. Fonda owned a large part of the show, and his face was seen not only as Simon Fry on NBC on Saturday nights, but also on the many products marketed while the show was on the air, including toy badges and guns, a paperback tie-in, a board game by Milton Bradley, and a comic book series by Dell.

Whatever angst the series might have brought to those who thought series television to be beneath a star of Fonda's stature, it is also true that *The Deputy* brought Henry Fonda into the living rooms of millions of Americans who never had the chance to see him at his apex, on stage, in *Mister Roberts*, from 1948- 1951. Millions of people, who loved Fonda in his westerns, whether it was *My Darling Clementine* or *The Tin Star*, got to see him in another one. And they were thrilled.

The Deputy represents an as yet largely untold story in the professional life of one of America's most admired and beloved stars. A sometimes difficult man in private life, Fonda was nevertheless loved by fans around the world. He was in many respects the face of the mid-twentieth century American man, and while he himself tended at times to put down some of his own work in the visual arts, the fact remains that his screen career included some of the most memorable roles in film history.

This is not to suggest, by any stretch of the imagination, that as a piece of art or popular culture *The Deputy* stands there with *The Grapes of Wrath* or *12 Angry Men*-- far from it. But in terms of screen time Fonda spent far more time on film, and was seen by more people, as Simon Fry, chief marshal of the Arizona Territory in *The Deputy*, than by those who saw him in many of his films or stage plays.

This was a fact that Fonda himself recognized about television at the time. He would recall, "I'd been on Broadway with *Mister Roberts* for four years to packed houses every night. And, every now and then, someone would recognize me on the street. Then I did *The Petrified Forest* with Humphrey Bogart and Lauren Bacall [on TV]. The next day, everybody—and I mean everybody, from the policemen to the truck driver—had seen me and knew me. I suddenly realized that I had gotten a bigger audience that one night than in four years of *Mister Roberts*." [8]

For that reason alone *The Deputy* is worthy of consideration of its place in Fonda's career, and its place in the history of the western on television.

It is also valuable to look at *The Deputy* in terms of its place in the history of television programming and production. It was part of a shift in Hollywood production patterns in the 1950s that saw many established Hollywood stars make the transition to television—Fonda was not the first but he was by far the biggest—and the series tried a different style production schedule, one meant to accommodate Fonda's schedule. It was an idea whose practical application was later perfected by Don Fedderson's company while producing *My Three Sons* with Fred MacMurray.

Finally, it should also be noted that *The Deputy* was the first television series to connect the words "created by" and "Norman Lear" in the credits. Lear and his writing partner and friend, Roland Kibbee, created the show, not wanting to miss a chance to work with Henry Fonda. Lear did not have as much contact with this western series that he would with his later, more famous, television series, but the fact remains that it was an important stepping stone in the career of a man whose talents changed the face of television in the 1970s.

The day before *The Deputy* premiered on NBC, Cecil Smith wrote in *The Los Angeles Times* that the show was "a delight and should be one of the major hits of the year… It's a western that is articulate and, at times, extremely funny. And with Fonda, how can you miss?" [9]

The series didn't miss when Fonda was fully engaged with Allen Case in episodes; on the contrary, many of the Fonda episodes are highly entertaining television westerns. The series did misfire at times in its selection of storylines and in figuring out credible and believable ways to keep the Fonda character relevant when Simon Fry wasn't heavily involved in the story. (Fry, it seemed, was too often walking into the marshal's office and then out again—and out of the story.) It was a problem fellow Hollywood star Robert Taylor didn't have on his first television series, which premiered in October 1959. Even though Taylor didn't make full appearances in every episode of *The Detectives Starring Robert Taylor*, his Matt Holbrook was at least seen handing out assignments to his detectives, not walking out of the room, and the episode, literally and figuratively.

Truth be told, when this series has been remembered at all, it has not always been fondly recalled or embraced by television critics and historians, Henry Fonda's fans, historians of the Western genre in film and television, or even Fonda himself. The BFI Companion to the Western, for example, called the series "something of a cheat" [10] because of Fonda's limited appearances. Fonda once referred to the series as "that terrible series at Revue." [11]

This book posits a different point of view entirely—that even though Fonda's decision to limit his appearances in *The Deputy* was and remains frustrating, his work in this series should not be ignored in his body of work. Instead, it should be watched, studied, and considered right alongside the other parts of his career. Fans should be thrilled that there are additional hours of Fonda's work to enjoy, instead of dismissing the program away as an aberration. It was and is another opportunity to watch Fonda work, with the added bonus of seeing him take a young actor under his wing.

Henry Fonda described his autobiography as a look at his life "warts and all." There is no reason to accept a different standard for this examination of his first weekly television series. Here, then, is the story of a television western—Henry Fonda, Allen Case, Read Morgan, Wallace Ford, and Betty Lou Keim in *The Deputy*.

CHAPTER TWO

Fondas and Non-Fondas

"He's a good man. I guess he'd have to be, naturally,
since I'm playing him, right?"

— Henry Fonda, describing Simon Fry [12]

Henry Fonda never quite understood his public image as a western star. "I don't mind that," he said in a 1975 interview on the BBC. "And I've done my share and I guess I've been lucky that some of those were the good ones ... and they're remembered. I'm not western, even with my accent. I'm from the middle west of the states, but cowboy? Forget it. I don't like horses. I don't like riding. They have to pay me a lot of money to get me on a horse." [13]

On another occasion he said, "I'm not much good on a horse. But I have to try to look good. I like to think it's not my fault. It's the fault of the horse.

"It looks so simple. There I am, and there's the horse at the hitching post, and there's the camera. But the instant I untie the horse and swing around to mount, the horse begins to back away. There he is with his tail in the cameraman's face, and I'm on the other side of him somewhere, and then the director yells disgustedly, 'Cut!'" [14]

He'd say in interviews that he only ever made a few westerns among his many films. But the public had long since strongly identified him with the genre by the time he began thinking about making a television western series in 1959.

Fonda's Westerns to the moment included *The Trail of the Lonesome Pine* (1936), *Jesse James* (1939), *Drums Along the Mohawk* (1939), *The Return of Frank James* (1940), *Wild Geese Calling* (1941), *The Ox-Bow Incident* (1943), *My Darling Clementine* (1946), *Fort Apache* (1948), *The Tin Star* (1957), and *Warlock* (1959).

As the highly-fictionalized Wyatt Earp in *My Darling Clementine*, Fonda had fashioned a truly memorable film portrayal. He simply was the western hero, and, as Tom Ryall pointed out in *The BFI Companion to the Western*, "The Wyatt Earp image sticks, however, probably because it lines up more closely with Fonda's most famous non- western roles in films such as *The Grapes of Wrath* and *Twelve Angry Men*." [15]

By the time Henry Fonda starred in *The Deputy*, he had for two decades represented American integrity, simplicity, and honesty on stage and on the silver screen.

"For a long time, I thought he could be our finest indigenous American actor," Norman Lear said of Fonda. "There was something about him, and John Wayne, that was so American." [16]

Director Peter Bogdanovich called Henry Fonda a national treasure, saying that "believability is a special quality of real stars and no one had it more than Fonda." [17]

Actor Read Morgan, who co- starred in the second season of *The Deputy*, said Fonda "was a prince of a guy." [18]

Henry Fonda was born on May 16, 1905, in Grand Isle, Nebraska, descended from the Dutch settlers who had founded the Upstate

New York town of Fonda. His family moved to Omaha before his first birthday. He enrolled at the University of Minnesota intending to be a newspaperman but dropped out after his sophomore year.

In 1925, while working at a credit company in Omaha, he ap-

Henry Fonda as Marshal Simon Fry. (Photofest)

peared as an actor for the first time, on stage at the Omaha Community Playhouse. Eventually, he found his way to Falmouth, MA, where he performed in summer stock starting in 1928 with the University Players, a group whose members included, at one time or another, Joshua Logan, James Stewart, and Margaret Sullavan.

His first part on Broadway came in 1929, his first Hollywood film (*The Farmer Takes a Wife*) in 1934. From there, as the saying goes, the rest is history. Henry Fonda, a son of Nebraska, would become one of the leading actors in the history of stage and filmmaking, creating memorable portrayal after memorable portrayal, from a young Abraham Lincoln (1939's *Young Mr. Lincoln*) to a seasoned military leader (as Admiral Nimitz in 1976's *Midway*). Fonda eventually earned a Lifetime Achievement Award from the American Film Institute (1978), the Kennedy Center Honors (1979), an honorary Academy Award (1981), and an Academy Award (1982) for his work in *On Golden Pond*, among numerous other career laurels.

Interviewed in 1960, director Sidney Lumet, who had directed Fonda in *12 Angry Men* and *Stage Struck*, said, "Hank Fonda, to me, is one of the most underestimated actors. If I read one more review that says 'Hank Fonda gave his usual good realistic performance,' I'll flip, because this man has such depth and such a sense of truth in his work—extraordinary." [19] Lumet directed Fonda again in 1964's *Fail-Safe*.

Fonda worked until his health permitted him to no longer; his final role in front of film cameras was shot back on Cape Cod, Massachusetts, where he had worked early in his career. The made for television film was *Summer Solstice* (1981), the result of a screenwriting competition sponsored by WCVB-TV in Boston. Henry Fonda died August 12, 1982.

Fonda always connected with the people, those cab drivers who kept asking him when he was going to make another western. Peter Bogdanovich wrote, "...his Lincoln, his Mister Roberts...his Tom Joad, have immortalized him—with such few others as James Stewart, Gary Cooper, and John Wayne—as a somehow more learned, yet equally individual aspect of The American. Because it was the Nebraska upbringing that kept him accessible to the heartland of the country..." [20]

The Americana image was further enhanced by his appearances in Westerns on network radio programs, including two more stints as Wyatt Earp. The first was the "Kansas Marshal" episode of *The Cavalcade of America* on March 31, 1947; the second was just a few weeks later, on *The Lux Radio Theatre,* in an adaptation of "My Darling Clementine" on April 28. Other radio appearances which solidified his image as a Western hero were "The Return of Frank James" on *Hollywood Star Time* on March 10, 1946; "Drums along the Mohawk" on *The Cavalcade of America* broadcast of November 10, 1941; and the February 2, 1941 episode of *The Gulf Screen Guild Theatre,* an adaptation of the motion picture "Destry Rides Again." [21]

Published star biographies often overlook the network radio appearances actors made in the 1930s, 1940s, and 1950s. Radio's place as the dominant mass medium was so quickly supplanted by television that its impact and importance in daily life in this country is too often forgotten and overlooked. But for researchers and historians, the lack of attention to these credits is remarkably shortsighted. These radio programs, *Lux* in particular, were heard by millions and millions of listeners across the country [22] and, when combined with Fonda's film appearances, cemented his image in the public mind as a star associated with the Western, bemused by the image though he may have been.

Fonda as Simon Fry, 1959. (Photofest)

Given his feelings on the subject, it might therefore appear to be somewhat surprising that of all the television series offers he had in the 1950s, Henry Fonda chose a western for his vehicle. But in 1959 network television was gripped by a frenzy of Westerns. Fonda's agents told him, "There are going to be more and more westerns on television forever and ever." [23]

"My agents sort of talked me into doing television," Fonda said. "It's their job to put a buck in the bank for me." [24]

Fonda's agents put that buck in the bank in this instance by securing a stake in the production. "I'm the co- owner, with the producers," Fonda said just before the series premiere. "And we chose a Western because obviously it's the most popular type series right now." He was a fifty-percent owner of the show, and formed his own production company, Top Gun, to run it. [25]

"We looked at a lot of ideas, of course, but when I saw the pilot script for *The Deputy*, this was the one I wanted to do," Fonda said. "I liked the character." [26]

Fonda did prefer to keep busy, and it's not as if he had shied away from television before on artistic grounds. While playing Simon Fry in *The Deputy* was Fonda's first starring role in a weekly series, he was hardly new to the medium. He had been making guest appearances on comedy and variety shows for as long as there had been network television, on programs such as *Tonight on Broadway* (1948, performing scenes from *Mister Roberts*), *Showtime USA* (two episodes in October 1950), *The Ed Sullivan Show* (four episodes between 1952 and 1957), *The Steve Allen Show* (two episodes in 1958), *The George Gobel Show* (one episode on October 11, 1959, dressed as Simon Fry in a western satire), and *The Sunday Showcase* (one episode in October,

Fonda and George Gobel, 1959. (Milton T. Moore Photos)

1959). And there were appearances in dramatic roles, as well— in an adaptation of Sinclair Lewis' "The Decision at Arrowsmith" for *The Medallion Theatre* in 1953; playing Emmett Kelly in "The Clown" for *The General Electric Theatre* in 1955 (an episode he also produced); and the now-famous *Producer's Showcase* production of "The Petrified Forest" in 1955 alongside Humphrey Bogart and Lauren Bacall.

Fonda had even hosted a weekly series in 1955, an anthology produced by Four Star and syndicated under several different names, including *Henry Fonda Presents the Star and the Story.* While Fonda said in one interview that he found it awkward to speak directly into the camera as host, [27] he did front the beer commercials for the show. "They showered me with gold," he said later. "I should've turned 'em down—but I didn't." [28] That gold was his fee for hosting the show-- $150,000. Fonda also took a few on the chin from critics ready to roast him for hosting the show.

His stated public regret at performing in the beer commercials notwithstanding, Fonda appeared in advertisements fairly often in his career, from the 1930s all the way to the late 1970s. He appeared in magazine advertisements in the 1940s and early 1950s for products including Schaefer Beer, Camel Cigarettes, and Arrow Shirts; later, there'd be a seven-year contract to serve as television spokesman for GAF products such as the Viewmaster and floor tiles in the 1960s and 1970s. Fonda also expressed regret at the GAF commercials: "It's a problem to find something that doesn't make you sick to your stomach. I sweated through seven years with GAF and was not unhappy when we quit."[29]

The television commercials for Kellogg's in 1959 had Fonda in costume as Simon Fry from *The Deputy,* standing in an old west general store.

Once news was out that Fonda had committed to a weekly television series, many people, friends included, wondered why. Fonda was always quite candid that it was the lure of cash upfront, and the residual payments, that helped to attract him. "Residuals are the checks you get when they sell the reruns and the work is all finished but the money keeps coming in. It's the only way an actor can make a substantial pile of dough to keep." [30]

Fonda also made no bones about the fact that he was interested in what he described as the "novel production formula" developed for the series—he shot almost all of his first season sequences for *The Deputy* in about ten weeks time in late summer and early fall, finishing up by the third week of October, freeing him up to begin rehearsals of *Silent Night, Lonely Night,* his next Broadway play.

"It was almost like a summer job for him," Read Morgan said. [31]

The only bump in this schedule came when the show's format changed that first year, requiring a few additional days work. Fonda would star in only six of the season's episodes, making only brief appearances in all the rest. Fonda liked that better, especially given his concern over being too strongly identified with a continuing character. "These TV actors are better known by their character names than by their real names. Even when they appear as the guest of another show, doing something different, they're identified as the series' characters." [32]

On the set, the episodes would become known as "Fondas" and "Non Fondas." In the "Fondas," the character of Simon Fry would play a pivotal role and appear all the way through the episode; in the "Non Fondas," Fry would have at least one major scene but would appear relatively little (sometimes very little), leaving the bulk of the work in the episode to co-star Allen Case, as Clay McCord, the local

NBC publicists described this shot as Fry
restraining his eager deputy. (Photofest)

storekeeper who is opposed to violence but is a crack shot and is often tricked into deputy duty.

Fonda could shoot "Non Fondas" at the rate of about five episodes a day. [33]

As the series premiered, Fonda did his best to defend the decision to limit his appearances, as well as explain it. "That may or may not sound like a hell of a lot, but actually I am in every one of the episodes. The very least I do comes to a little over a page and a half of dialogue in one of the segments. Believe me, we're not trying to cheat anybody. I've talked this over with the people with whom I'm producing the show, and we hashed out a lot of details and problems." [34]

It was further decided that Fonda's character would narrate most episodes as a way to both move the storylines forward and give the appearance of deeper involvement by Fry.

"This sounds like cheating," Fonda admitted, "but it really isn't. The brief appearances are done in such a way that you have the feeling that this marshal, my character, is actively involved all the time. Anyway, the sponsors are satisfied that they're getting Fonda and not just a teaser to trick the audience." [35]

But Fonda's brief appearances in the other thirty-three episodes of the first season did cause consternation among the fans of The *Deputy*," especially in that first half- season in the fall of 1959. One such frustrated fan told *TV Guide* that "In walks Fonda, he says 'Howdy,' he leaps on his horse and you don't see him again until the end of the show." [36]

"I understand there has been a disappointed reaction from people who want more of *me*," Fonda told one interviewer. "I can only say I'm glad they want me, but they're not going to get me that much." [37]

The third episode of the series, "Back to Glory," would demonstrate the basic format the producers devised to try to showcase the Simon Fry character even when he wasn't fully involved in the story. In this episode, Fry appears in the first act, expressing outrage and concern for a woman who's been attacked and raped by outlaws. When Fry discovers that there was another woman in the party, he goes off to find her. Fry is not seen again until the end of the episode, when it is revealed that he took ill and had spent time in bed, while the characters of Clay McCord and Herk Lamson managed to track down the outlaws. Fonda/Fry flashes his famous grin before the end credits roll.

Normally in a television series, this kind of episode would be one way producers could temporarily write around a major character to give other characters more screen time. But for *The Deputy*, this was the norm in almost all of the episodes, and millions of viewers who had been looking forward to seeing Fonda in a weekly series were enormously frustrated and disappointed.

"We never pretended anything except what we were doing," Fonda said. "Every story that went out—anybody that interviewed me, Allen Case, or anybody else—knew that I was only going to be involved in six of the thirty-nine, and in the other thirty-three, in a very small way. I never pretended otherwise.

"We didn't try to make the audience expect more. But a lot of people who don't read the publicity releases probably did think they were going to see me in every segment." [38]

And the truth was, "Back to Glory" was one of the better examples of a "Non Fonda" in the series—Simon Fry does feel integrated into the story. The Fonda grin covered up for a lot. But in many other episodes, the absence of Fonda was keenly felt, and the insertion of Fry was contrived, to say the least.

Take the episode "Final Payment," episode 26 of season one, broadcast March 19, 1960, as one example. In this episode, Clay battles a vengeful man who has taken over the mortgage to the general store and wants to put Clay out of business. Clay's sister Fran sends for Simon Fry, but Clay rides out to meet Fry on the prairie, long before Fry gets to Silver City, and convinces Fry to turn around. The scene between Fonda and Case takes place in the middle of the episode, and this is all the viewer sees of Fry in "Final Payment," until a file footage shot of Fonda riding across the prairie is run with a quick voice-over narration at the close.

Logistically, the one scene in this episode was a dream come true for the producers because it was between only Fonda and Case, and made for easy production scheduling. That's one of the reasons why many of Fonda's scenes in the "Non Fondas" are with Allen Case or one of the other regulars and not guest stars. Fonda's work in this episode took just part of a day to complete, and totaled about five pages of script. [39]

"The idea of *The Deputy*, of course, is to give a great deal of the play to the marshal's deputy," Fonda said. "We tested a lot of young actors and settled on Allen Case. He's always associated with the marshal, you see. The marshal is always 'there,' even when you don't actually see him. His presence is just felt; that's the best way I can explain it." [40]

The explanation didn't assuage all the fans. The format became, as one news report described it, "a prime target for criticism." [41] Fonda was just out to make a buck, so went the criticism, by lending his name to the series.

But co-star Wallace Ford, a Hollywood veteran, said there was another side to the discussion that people were missing. "Fonda staked his whole career on this kid," Ford said. "I think it should be fairly obvious that the only reason he put his name on the show was to sell it so this Case kid could have his chance.

"Case has never even been in a picture before, but he's got it. Fonda saw to that. I think Fonda is to be commended, not criticized. Television's always crying for new talent. So here it is, and Fonda put it on. More stars should have the courage to dig up talent like that and use their names to sell it.

"Fonda believes in this kid. Time and time again I've heard him tell the directors, 'Don't put this shot on me. Keep the camera on the kid. He's the one.'" [42]

The "novel production formula" was not without its problems. For the crew of Top Gun, it was a constant challenge of organization and continuity. Many unanticipated problems came up.

"We soon found," Fonda said, "That if I were to shoot not only my six episodes but all my other appearances in advance, early enough to cut me loose for rehearsals of a play I had agreed to do, we were going to have problems.

"First, we had to get all of the scripts way ahead of time. Then, if I did a brief scene with an actor who also was to appear in the rest of the film, we'd have to gamble on his being available five or six weeks later when they got around to shooting the rest of it. If we shot those other scenes within four weeks of his first call, we'd have to pay him for…'holding' him and keeping him unavailable for other shows. Very expensive." [43]

The production challenges continued in the second season, when actor Read Morgan was brought on board to play Hapgood Tasker, a cavalry sergeant. "We had to shoot everything in the summer time that Fonda was going to be in. We did thirteen heavy Fonda segments,

**Simon Fry (Henry Fonda) questions suspects (played by
Dennis Patrick and Clarke Alexander) in "Focus of Doom,"
a first season "Fonda." (Western TV Photos)**

and then Allen and I would go around the rest of the year, and finish up the show.

"We were shooting so fast. We'd start a show on Monday morning and Wednesday after lunch we'd start another show. We were shooting two shows a week and then we were off a week." [44]

Morgan said the production schedule was a tremendous coordination challenge from a script standpoint. "They had to have all the 39 shows in scripts when they first started shooting. And that's why a lot of those actors had one-day parts because they might work one day when Hank was in town and they might work one day six months later when he wasn't." [45]

Every so often, the quirks of the production schedule would create a need to change a line in a script, or a scene to be re-edited. In the first-season episode "Final Payment," for example, the original script called for Herk Lamson to send a wire asking Simon for help. That was later changed to Fran asking for the chief marshal's help, and a campfire scene between Simon and Clay had to be re-edited removing references to Herk Lamson.

It was also true that in his work for the series Fonda found a certain creative challenge. "The challenge to create an exciting characterization has always intrigued me both as an actor and as a member of the entertainment industry," he said in a syndicated newspaper column attributed to him that September, as the show readied for its premiere. "Moving between two such lively mediums as television, where an actor is exposed to an enormous audience in a single performance, and the stage, where he can refresh his sense of timing and rapport with a live, intimate audience, enables the performer to maintain a true perspective in his work." [46]

To another interviewer, Fonda said, "It's as much a challenge as any movie or stage play I ever did. An actor who doesn't appreciate what television can offer is behind the times." [47]

Read Morgan scoffs at any suggestion that Fonda didn't give the series his best effort. "He was the consummate pro. You could shoot his rehearsals. You never had to call for him. He was always on the set." [48]

The Deputy set was a happy one, according to director Tay Garnett, who emerged as a major director of second-season episodes. Garnett told a story that certainly belies any notion that Fonda was disengaged from the work. "I was always there at 8:00," Garnett wrote. "Invariably, Hank Fonda was ahead of me, lounging loosely in a canvas chair as if he were strictly a passenger. However, he managed to be near the stage door as other members of the cast arrived. To each he'd say a few words, and they would sit down together.

"My curiosity prompted me to check up. One person to whom I talked said, 'Well, this is confidential, but Hank admitted he hadn't had time to study his script, so he wanted me to work with him over our scene.'"

Garnett continued: "That'll be the day, when Hank hadn't learned his lines! The result was that when I was ready to shoot, Hank had rehearsed the entire cast. We always finished our segments well ahead of schedule." [49]

The show started off in September and October of 1959 with good reviews and respectable ratings. (It should have—Wallace Ford said $130,000 was spent on the pilot, an unheard of sum for a pilot in those years.) [50] Cecil Smith, writing in *The Los Angeles Times*, said, "It's easy to see the high promise in a look at the pilot—the realism and the gun fighting are tempered with bright, articulate dialogue, reasonable plots, and the superb skill of Fonda as an actor." [51]

Fonda thought highly of the pilot, "Badge for a Day," as well. "The pilot was just great," he said. "There was a lot of excitement over it. Less than twenty-four hours after the print was shown in New York, it was bought, by Kellogg's, incidentally. The word had gotten out that we had a big one on the open market." [52]

The pilot was written by series creators Roland Kibbee and Norman Lear, and directed by Don Medford. Medford brought thirteen years experience in television and film to the set in 1959, and he was no stranger to working with big-time Hollywood names, either. In 1959 alone, he directed segments of various television series starring Fonda, Bette Davis, Ray Milland, and Joan Crawford.

Broadcasting reviewed the series premiere and called the series "The best new western of the season," but wondered what impact Fonda's absence would have the series. *Variety* noted that "despite the known fact that Fonda, cast as a chief marshal, will eventually be lending more of his name than his energies to *The Deputy,* stanza has another asset, a new, young actor, Allen Case." [53]

So it proved as the series got further underway. Fonda also starred in the fourth episode, Roland Kibbee's excellent "Shadow of the Noose," and made brief appearances in episodes two and three, "The Wild Wind" and "Back to Glory," and the ratings were good. Fonda was even congratulated on the authenticity of his "western slouch," but he told an interviewer, "That's no western slouch. I've been round-shouldered all my life."[54]

Fonda maintained that the sponsor was pleased with the early episodes. "Well, it's one thing to make a good pilot and then goof off for the rest of the series, but hear this. The agency saw about five installments thus far and they are ecstatic. As for myself, I'll keep on top of the series and take charge as long as my commitments allow." [55]

But, the ratings slumped for several weeks in the first season as audience disillusionment over the Fonda/Non Fonda issue grew. The pilot had set a high standard and, as in all television, not all episodes were living up to the promise, although many were entertaining.

Later, Fonda would say, "You get seduced by the pilot script. The first few scripts are excellent, and then the writer that sold you on the series moves on to something else. They start farming out the scripts to different writers, and you begin to fight the scripts, to fight the producers. You either throw away the scripts, or you do bad shows." [56]

Slowly but surely, however, the ratings rebounded, as the audience grew more acclimated with the format. When Robert Montgomery, Jr. guest-starred as a troubled teenager wounded in an attempted bank robbery in "The Two Faces of Bob Claxton" on February 27, 1960, one critic wrote that "The Deputy emerges as a fresh breeze out of the well-trodden shoot 'em up corral." [57] By the time "The X Game" aired on May 28, 1960, toward the end of the season, one critic was even suggesting that "This would be a far better series if Chief Marshal Henry Fonda didn't show up for a few minutes each week to delay Deputy Allen Case in the pursuit of his duties." [58]

At the end of the first season, NBC and Fonda committed to another season of shows, with a welcome twist for Fonda fans.

For season two, Fonda increased his workload to fully starring in thirteen episodes, rather than just six, a concession to audience expectations. "I'll appear in 13 stories all the way through," Fonda told *TV Guide*. "Maybe put in four months all told and still be able to do other things. I'll appear briefly in all of them, just the way I did this season." And in a nod to his co-star, Allen Case, Fonda said, "Figure maybe I'd better. This kid Case is getting too good." [59]

In assessing Henry Fonda and *The Deputy*, discussion of the relative quality of the "Fondas" versus the "Non Fondas" is inevitable. In his book, *Riding the Video Range: The Rise and Fall of the Western on Television*, Gary Yoggy described the problem as "Two distinct levels of quality. The 'Fonda episodes' are significantly better than the others. His charisma is apparent even on the home screen, and there is authority and integrity in his portrayal of the veteran Western lawman. Furthermore, the scenes between Fonda and Case are intense ... The episodes Case carries lack this tension and chemistry." [60]

Allen Case, who in his first starring role on television acquitted himself extremely well, was popular with the fans of the show, and carried himself professionally. But the audience simply wanted as much Fonda as it could get. That an episode would be better because Fonda was in it is self-explanatory, and the fans could hardly be blamed for wanting more Fonda.

The show was heavily marketed by NBC as a Fonda show. "Henry Fonda Starring in *The Deputy*" was the advertising featured in publicity shots, in artwork on weekly television program magazines, in local and national newspapers, and even on shopping bags in some grocery stores. The image of Fonda was prominent on all of the tie-in products associated with the series, including toy guns, comic books, and postcards. It's understandable that the public would be expecting a heavier Fonda presence than what was received.

Still, some of the most interesting episodes produced during this golden age of the television western were seen as part of the run of *The Deputy*, thanks in large part to the presence of Henry Fonda. There are marvelous moments in the series featuring Fonda as Simon Fry, the kind of little moments that give narrative television its strength.

In "The Means and the End," for example, broadcast on March 18, 1961 as the 25th episode of season two, Fry holds a woman prisoner in the Silver City jail and threatens to hang her. The marshal is really using her as bait to lure in her outlaw husband, and the scheme works. When Simon Fry confronts the outlaw in the street and says, "You mean to interfere with the law?," [61] it is frontier justice being served in a storyline that was unique—a marshal using a woman as bait. This wasn't something viewers would necessarily have seen other marshals or sheriffs do on other television westerns of the time.

Many of the "Non Fonda" segments also stand as very entertaining episodes. In "The Last Gunfight," from April 30, 1960, Allen Case is in top form as Clay tries to help a reformed gunfighter who wants to leave his past behind. When the gunfighter is killed by two younger gunslingers, Clay and Fry decide to list the cause of death as a single bullet from an unknown assailant to prevent either of the young men from taking credit and further spreading violence. Fry's closing narration is as a fitting bookend: "Funny thing—you'd expect a fast draw like Clay McCord to handle a gunslinger's problem with his gun. Instead of which he used his head and his heart and I ain't seen the day when a gun could do as well." [62]

A second season Non Fonda episode, "An Enemy of the Town," illustrates the series' attempt to at least try something different. In this Ibsenesque story, Clay threatens to shut down a local tannery because he believes it may be polluting the water supply. But in a moment rare to the television western, Clay McCord, a heroic figure on the series, someone who generally fought for the future and didn't accept things as they were, gave in to demands from local businessmen to reopen it:

The hero in *The Deputy* took an active part in a crusade
to stop the polluting of a stream despite protests by the
community. However, it is interesting that he 'gave up'
the fight when he was near victory—as though he were
unfamiliar with the role of the active participant in a fight
against things as they are. [63]

This was a fascinating display of human weakness on the part of
Clay McCord, and Clay was made all the more heroic when he recovered his bearings and took up the fight again.

Over the course of the series, the audience eventually made its
peace with the Fonda/Non Fonda issue. "The show seems to be clicking," Case said in the spring of 1960. [64] Eventually, NBC was even
ready to order a third season of episodes; as late as April 1961, executives were talking with Fonda about renewing the series and bumping
the episodes up to an hour.

But Fonda pulled the plug, saying his other work commitments
wouldn't permit him to devote himself to the rigors of the television
production schedule. At a time when *Gunsmoke* was moving to an
hour-long format and other series were considering it, *The Deputy*
came to an end.

"With the hour-long shows seeming to be the trend this year, I
was asked to expand *The Deputy* into a sixty-minute show." Fonda
wrote. "That would mean, therefore, that at least nine months of the
year would have to be spent in Hollywood filming the shows, which
would preclude any other motion picture or stage activity." [65]

"We could have been *Bonanza* or any of those things, as long as

Fonda wanted to do it," Read Morgan said. "But we shot a half-hour show in two-and-a-half days, so we were shooting like a machine gun. And the speed and the quality was just not what Hank was used to, and so at the end of two years he got enough of it because he was still doing Broadway shows and he was still doing movies." [66]

Morgan said the cancellation came so fast that one day he had a parking spot and a dressing room on the lot and the next day he didn't.

Fonda moved on, Morgan said, even though he'd been told that with one more year on the show, and a starring role in thirteen more episodes, he'd be able to sell out his half of the show for a million dollars. "Hank didn't need the money. He was more interested in doing what he wanted to do, which at that stage of his career you can't blame him." [67]

The summer following the end of *The Deputy*, Fonda shot his sequences in the Cinerama film *How the West Was Won* and was signed for *Advise and Consent* in 1962.

Years later, when prepping his second series, *The Smith Family*, Fonda would look back on *The Deputy* and say that one of the biggest problems on the series was the scripts, and that he had to compromise every day. He said often the scripts wouldn't be ready until the day of shooting, which was not, he said, any way to run a series. "The scripts used to arrive about the same time as the actors. You never knew what you were doing until you did it, good or bad, and it was too late to do anything about it." [68]

Fonda never did quite adjust to the speed of production. He told one interviewer that he gave up smoking king-size cigarettes while filming the series because he only had time to smoke regulars. [69]

But it would be disingenuous to say Fonda necessarily thought less of

The Deputy than he did of much of his other work in films and on television. While his later comments indicate he had found some of the series work frustrating, he spoke differently in 1961, as the series was wrapping up. "I enjoyed the two years that I was doing the series," he said in one newspaper column attributed to him. "Certainly there are pressures, but I must say I was very impressed with the way they keep on a schedule. I think the theatre and films could learn a lesson from the technicians in television." [70]

Henry Fonda's first love, after all, was the theatre—much of the rest was simply work. He openly disparaged many of his films. He returned to the stage again and again in his long career. Coming into production of *The Deputy*, Fonda was coming off four straight Broadway hits, a remarkable achievement. From 1948- 1959, he starred in *Mister Roberts* (1948- 1951), *Point of No Return* (1951- 1952), *The Caine Mutiny Court Martial* (1954- 1955), and *Two for the Seesaw* (1958). Once the series was underway, Fonda continued on stage, in *Silent Night, Lonely Night* (December 3, 1959- March 19, 1960) and *Critic's Choice* (December 14, 1960- March 19, 1961).

While Fonda would not count *The Deputy* among his most memorable work, several episodes of the series, including "Badge for a Day," "Hang the Law," and "Shadow of the Noose" (see chapter five), are among the best of their genre, and his work as Simon Fry in these episodes ranks high on the list of Fonda western characterizations.

Fonda's full presence in those nineteen episodes gives those episodes a stature unmatched by other series.

"I was so lucky, at that age, to be able to work with someone who was the consummate pro that he was," Read Morgan said. [71]

And then there were the horses. One Friday afternoon, early in the history of the series, Fonda pulled up on a horse on the back lot at Revue, dismounted, and said, "If this was a detective series, the lot would be crawling with pretty dames. In a western, what do you get—horses!" [72]

CHAPTER THREE

A Cast of Characters and Crew

HENRY FONDA as Marshal Simon Fry

To say that the presence of Henry Fonda brought immediate attention and prestige to the public image of *The Deputy* is something of an
understatement. Fonda was hardly the first well-known Hollywood
star to agree to star in a weekly television series—indeed, at the time
Fonda signed for *The Deputy*, stars such as June Allyson, Joel McCrea,
and Robert Taylor were also signing for their own series. All were
immensely popular stars for years -- but they were not known as
top-shelf caliber actors in the sense that Fonda was. Fonda had been
nominated for an Academy Award for *Young Mister Lincoln* and had
won a Tony Award for *Mister Roberts*.

The idea that a major film star would take on a series was new to
television in the late 1950s, but was it was old hat in network radio.
Alan Ladd (*Box 13*), James Stewart (*The Six Shooter*), Humphrey Bogart and Lauren Bacall (*Bold Venture*), and Tyrone Power (*Freedom*

USA) are just a few of the stars who'd been in front of the public in a weekly radio series before. Of course, the production schedule of a radio series was far less demanding on a star's time than a television series would be, as the performers could record their lines into a recorder between takes on a film set if need be.

In television, many series leads were performed by actors who had often taken secondary leads in films, such as Ralph Bellamy and Eve Arden, who were major television stars in the fifties in *Man Against Crime* and *Our Miss Brooks*, respectively. But whether it was because of studio resistance or more personal reasons, it wasn't until the latter part of the decade that major stars turned an eye toward headlining a series, rather than just making occasional guest appearances. [73]

Now, television had landed one of the biggest.

Fonda may indeed have taken on the role of Simon Fry "somewhat reluctantly," as his biographer Howard Teichmann described it, [74] but it remains that Fonda's enormous standing with the public, his public identification with the Western, his image as the embodiment of what it meant to be American, and his solid performances gave the series legitimacy in the very crowded field of westerns on network television in 1959.

Simon Fry stood for law and order in the Arizona Territory of 1880. He was described as "fiercely devoted to his duty, relentless in pursuit of law breakers, asking and giving no quarter when facing desperadoes or killers." [75]

"That man lives for his work and nothing else," Fran McCord says in "Back to Glory." Clay answers, "It's a lucky thing for the rest of us, Fran." [76]

The character of Simon Fry is firmly rooted in the depiction of the traditional western hero in the television western, with a few notable

One of Hollywood's biggest stars comes to
weekly television. (Western TV Photos)

differences. Writing about the western hero, Don Kirkley noted that the lawman "may have had the respect of the townspeople, but often lacked their support in moments of crisis. Hence, he was often put in the position of having to face the forces of evil alone, performing almost superhuman feats of bravery in order to overcome these forces." [77]

Certainly, this was true of Simon Fry—he was a western hero cast from the same mold as Marshal Matt Dillon in *Gunsmoke*, or Marshal Wyatt Earp in *The Life and Legend of Wyatt Earp*. Fry shared the same sense of duty, the same quiet nature, the same sense of right and wrong, and the same belief in punishing injustice. As described in the series Writer's Presentation, Fry was "deadly with a gun and no lily with his fists...cool, fearless, but never reckless...soft of speech, quick to grin and joke, a smooth talker...a mischievous sense of humor." [78] But Fry, unlike these and other network television marshals, was often unshaved, tired, and short on money ("Fatal Urge" was one episode where Fry searched his pockets for money but couldn't find any)—a more realistic portrayal than some of television's other lawmen. In the episode titled "The Dream," Fry was even seen doing his laundry, hanging it to dry right in the middle of the Silver City marshal's office. When Blanche Niles, the matriarch of Ludlow in "Hang the Law," looks at the dirty and trail weary Fry and calls him a "gunfighter," it is not a compliment. [79]

Not surprisingly, Simon was also created with more than a little nod to Henry Fonda's public persona. While Fry was fast with his gun, he was not a servant to that gun. He was slow of speech but deliberate, and while he displayed determination in upholding the law, Simon was seen as simple and uncomplicated in his ways—what you saw was what you got from Simon Fry. Moreover, "he is not a big talker, although when dealing with felons or desperadoes he may be quick of tongue. His gait is, like his manner, deliberate and unique." [80]

Henry Fonda said Simon was "not glamorous, not by a long shot.

"He's not gimmicked up with props, trick guns, or what have you, and he doesn't wear fancy duds. As a matter of fact, the wardrobe is particularly good, realistic as all hell. Simon changes a shirt just one, I believe, in fifteen episodes.

"He covers a lot of territory, and can't be lugging a complete change of dress for dinner. All he's got is what's in his saddle pack, and that doesn't amount to much more than a bed roll, food staples, maybe some underwear, and ammunition.

"To top if off, when he's on the road, he's going to get a three-day growth of beard, good guy or no." [81]

Fry himself summed up the life of a lawman in a piece of narration from the episode "The Silent Gun," from January 23, 1960, in which Clay has sought out Fry's advice and has found him camped out for the night:

> "For a hard-workin' man with a clear conscience, the chief marshal sure don't find virtue bein' its own reward. Sleepin' with one eye open, suspicious of every sound and most strangers. So naturally, it pleasured me to see my good friend and occasional deputy Clay McCord comin' out of the darkness, even if he might be on nuthin' better than store business." [82]

Hard experience taught Fry to take all the help he could get, and he used any and all means to get the help he needed, especially from Clay McCord.

It is interesting to note about *The Deputy* that while Fry often was all that stood between law and disorder in these stories about the Arizona Territory, he was more than ably assisted by Clay McCord. Clay was younger and less experienced than Fry (Clay was about 24 years old in the series, Fry was 41), [83] but he was able to maintain the law in Silver City without Fry's help, giving this series two capable western heroes, instead of just one.

ALLEN CASE as Clay McCord

The star in *The Deputy* was Henry Fonda, but in almost every other way the star of *The Deputy* was Allen Case, then a relative unknown.

"He was a terrific actor," actress Kathy Garver said. "He got into his character with a sense of who the person actually was." [84]

Imagine what it must have been like for Allen Case in 1959, a young actor-singer, to not only be cast a co-star of a major prime-time network television series, but to be cast opposite Henry Fonda— Hollywood royalty, as Read Morgan described him. [85] It must have been exciting, thrilling—and daunting.

For all the talk of Henry Fonda's connection to the western, Allen Case really was from the West—Texas—and had horses in his yard when he was growing up. "We had horses in the backyard at home until I was almost in my teens," he said in a 1962 interview, [86] although he admitted in 1965 that as far as horses went, "In our family, it was the women, my mother and sister, who had the enthusiasm." [87]

The co-starring role next to a famous Hollywood and Broadway star came to Case, then in his mid-twenties, by accident. "I was out at Revue to test for a part that wasn't right for me in a Bill Bendix series [88]

Instead I was asked to test for *The Deputy* in the part which originally called for a much older man." [89]

"When we were casting for *The Deputy* I must have looked at hundreds of prospects," Fonda told *TV Guide*. "Then along came Allen. I

Allen Case as Clay McCord. (Western TV Photos)

can't tell you why this was our man any more than I can tell you why I like a play or a painting. You just have a feeling for people like him." [90]

Given the series format, the role of the storekeeper/deputy would require an actor who could carry the show in most of the episodes—all of those episodes Fonda didn't appear in full-time. Further, the actor was going to have to withstand a great deal of scrutiny given the inevitable comparison to the "Fonda" episodes.

"This kid," said Fonda in 1960, "not only has looks, ease and naturalness, but an authority without seeming presumptuous." [91]

Read Morgan recalled Case's naturalness before the camera. "One day somebody said to him, 'What are you doing, imitating Henry Fonda? And he said, can you think of a better guy to imitate?'" [92]

Morgan said Case dealt with the pressures well. "He was always cool and always came prepared and knew what he was doing." [93]

The Deputy was the first television series-starring role for Case; later, he would also star as older brother Frank James in *The Legend of Jesse James* for one season in 1965- 66, a role Fonda had played in two westerns, *Jesse James* and *The Return of Frank James.* Case had guest-starred on several series before landing the role of Clay McCord, including *Gunsmoke, Wagon Train, Have Gun, Will Travel,* and *The Rifleman,* and was well-acquainted with the Western genre.

Allen Case was born Allen Jones on October 8, 1934 in Dallas, Texas, the son of a retail clothier. He attended Southern Methodist University, and made the rounds of radio stations and other venues where he could showcase his fine singing voice. He eventually landed a five-week job on Arthur Godfrey's morning program in 1954; it was Godfrey who thought up the name "Allen Case." There were fears Allen Jones might be confused with the movie singer Allan Jones, and so they adopted "Case" from Allen's father, who was named Casey.

Of Godfrey, Case said, "I owe him a lot." [94]

The stint on the Godfrey show got Case a recording contract, but he said later the rock 'n roll songs Columbia gave him to sing were wrong for him. "I'm a ballad or musical comedy man. I just couldn't get with that rock 'n roll stuff. Neither could the record buyers." [95]

Case was far more successful with a record album that came out during the first season of *The Deputy* called "The Deputy Sings." The album contains ballads such as "I'll Be Seeing You" and "These Foolish Things." Case told *TV Guide*, "At last I'm doing the kind of things that are right for me." [96]

The right kind of things in music for Allen Case did not include western songs, be they country-western or even cowboy songs, and that's why, unfortunately, he never sang on *The Deputy*, a la Dean Martin in *Rio Bravo*.

In fact, he had hidden his singing career from the producers of *The Deputy* at the time of his audition. "I was afraid if I told them in advance I was a singer it might alter their thinking of me as an actor," he said. "But I haven't lost my appetite for musicals." [97]

Had *The Deputy* not been renewed for a second season, Case would have spent the summer of 1960 as host of the program filling in for the Garry Moore television show that year. Moore had selected Case as host for the show, but had to go looking elsewhere when Case went back to work on *The Deputy*. [98]

Case's theatrical experience in the '50s included the plays *Reuben, Reuben, Pleasure Dome, South Pacific*, and *Damn Yankees*. He even played nightclubs before the guest spots on TV westerns starting popping up—the first was an episode of *Bronco,* which aired September 23, 1958.

Case considered himself fortunate to have the role on *The Deputy,* and to be working with Henry Fonda. Case said Fonda had always been one of his favorites, although he didn't think it best to tell him so. "Hank and I get along fine," he said in the summer of 1960. "While my acting and interpretation differ from his, it is a pleasure to watch him in action." Case echoed what many other actors had said about Fonda: "His timing is superb." [99]

As for the Fonda/Non Fonda issue, Case was diplomatic in the middle of the series' first season. "A lot of little kids have the idea that I'm Fonda, but of course I'm not. He appears for about two minutes in the majority of sequences, but he does appear in the whole show six times. He'll be back from New York soon, where he's appearing in *Silent Night, Lonely Night.* No, the arrangement doesn't bother me at all." [100]

The Deputy and Allen Case premiered to generally good reviews. In *The New York Times,* for example, Jack Gould wrote on September 14, 1959, two days after the series premiere, that "Mr. Case, as the deputy, could catch on with the small fry." [101] This proved to be the case as the season progressed. "Much of the mail I get comes from teen- aged girls," Case said, "and they report that the whole family watches the series. They are glad that the hero is not a superman and the heavies are not all detestable animals." [102]

After the two-year run of *The Deputy,* Case played summer stock, rodeos, supper clubs, and county fairs, often singing. There was talk of another television series, a non- western, within a year after the end of *The Deputy,* but that didn't pan out. He made guest appearances in many more TV series during the 1960s, 1970s, and early 1980s, and co- starred, not always happily, in *The Legend of Jesse James* series at 20th Century-Fox for the 1965- 66 season. He continued his singing and theatrical career, starring, for example, as "Harvey" in the Tony Award-winning musical comedy *Hallelujah, Baby!* on Broadway in 1967 and 1968.

He had always been confident about his post-*Deputy* career. He told an interviewer in 1960, "I was in the entertainment business for several years before this series. I was in musical comedy for three and a half years, and I toured for 58 weeks with *Damn Yankees*. Oh, yes, *The Deputy* has meant a lot to me, but Allen Case will still be around when *The Deputy* is gone." [103] His later business ventures included the purchase of his father's retail store in Dallas and, in the late 1960s, designing fur coats for men.

In 1973, Case co-starred with Kathy Garver, best known for her role as Cissy on the television series *Family Affair*, in a dinner theater production of *The Ninety Day Mistress* in Florida. "He was entertaining, warm, and caring," Garver said. "Allen was professional, talented, and added an extra special something to his characters—whether it was his wry sense of humor or a behaviorism that flushed out his character." [104]

Sadly, Case's life was cut far too short. While vacationing in Truckee, California, in 1986, he suffered a heart attack, and died on August 25. He was only 51 years old. His last two television appearances had been on episodes of *Hill Street Blues* and *Chips* in 1981 and 1982, respectively.

"He died entirely too young and I will always remember his wit and wisdom," Garver said. [105]

Case had enjoyed playing Clay McCord and working with Henry Fonda. (Fonda would later ask for Case on a 1965 episode of *The Bell*

Allen Case tending to his other business
interests, behind the scenes. (Western TV Photos)

Telephone Hour he had originally been scheduled to host.) "Allen is going a long way," Fonda said in 1960. [106]

The two actors remained friends and stayed in contact throughout their lives. Case was called to Fonda's bedside a few days before Fonda died in 1982. Of working with Fonda, Case said in 1962, "He's a terribly talented man, and along with that he's kind as well as being a considerate and diligent worker." [107]

Similar words were often spoken about Allen Case. Betty Lou Keim said that he was a gentleman and that she had a special rapport with him. [108]

Case appeared in all but one of the 76 episodes of *The Deputy*, missing only "The Lonely Road" during the series' second season and said he appreciated the approach the series took on its storylines. "We always tell a story and don't resort to unnecessary brutality. [109] The plots are simple but they are not cliché—we hope.

"I started out on the show by being an expert with a gun, with a dislike for violence. I'm still expert but there have been a few episodes in which I wasn't even armed." [110]

Clay McCord was young, good looking, and rugged, but his strongest asset was his gentleness, even though he was known as the fastest gun in the territory. He refused to carry a gun, at least in the earliest episodes of the series, convinced as he was that side-arms would only lead to violence and killing. In fact, Clay did his best to avoid violence whenever possible, though he found himself repeatedly in situations requiring him to be violent to keep the peace. He even stored his handgun in a locked box with the word "poison" painted on it.

Clay's feelings were never better described than in the first season episode, "The Silent Gun," when Silver City Marshal Herk Lamson is hopeful that Clay will strap on both his guns and a badge because a gun-slinger has come to town. "If you take all the handguns away and pass a law makin' 'em illegal," Clay says, "this senseless killin' would stop." [111]

Clay's abhorrence of violence stemmed from his father's death—it was a violent one. His father, Luke, had thrived an excitement and danger and was unable to keep himself out of trouble, despite his deep love for his wife, Clay's mother Hester. Luke McCord is referred to in several episodes, including "The Silent Gun," as being a fast gun and as having taught Clay how to shoot. The Writers' Presentation described Luke McCord as:

> One of the most ingratiating, devil-may-care individuals on the raw frontier…Luke thrived on excitement and danger, seemed unable to avoid getting into tight spots. He was a brave man but a reckless one—a throwback to the ancient knights with their contempt for caution and their love for the joust. [112]

The general store in Silver City was started by Hester McCord as a way to support her children after her husband died; Clay and his sister Fran inherited the family business upon their mother's death. [113] Hester had long since stopped trying to tame her husband; instead, she tried to show her children "that the useful life was better than the carefree one." [114]

Clay's personality came from both his mother and his father—while he abhorred violence and went out of his way to avoid it; neither was he a man to shy away from responsibility and danger when presented with them.

Clay may have been the fastest gun in the territory, but what he wanted to do is run the general store to support his sister and his younger brother. His siblings became his responsibility upon the death of their parents.

Clay also served as the gunsmith of Silver City, repairing rifles and other guns, with the exceptions of side-arms.

Simon Fry sought Clay out whenever he needed a deputy to help with criminal elements and victims in and around Silver City. In the first-season episode "The Border Between," from March 12, 1960, Simon invites Clay boar hunting when in fact Simon needed his deputy's help to escort a prisoner back to Arizona Territory from Mexico. Clay suspected nearly every casual word of Marshal Fry because of past incidents in which he has been involved against his will in law enforcement. [115]

Later, Clay served as deputy marshal in Silver City, and carried a gun at all times, but was still reluctant to use violence except as a last resort. In second-season episodes, Clay McCord, now the deputy marshal of Silver City, stood for law and order and would stand up against any and all evildoers, but he also sought out, and often found, more peaceful resolutions to the conflicts confronting the people of Silver City in 1880.

BETTY LOU KEIM as Fran McCord

A Massachusetts native, Betty Lou Keim was born in the city of Malden, Massachusetts, just north of Boston, in 1938, and had already assembled impressive lists of theatrical, film, and television credits when she took on the role of Fran McCord, Clay McCord's younger sister, on *The Deputy*.

By the time cameras were rolling on the series pilot, Keim had been working for fourteen years. She had made her professional debut on stage in 1945 as "young Laura Dean" in the Broadway adaptation of *Strange Fruit,* directed and produced by Jose Ferrer. The production ran for sixty performances between November 1945 and January, 1946, and Keim's career was off to the races.

A role in another Broadway play, 1947's *Crime and Punishment,* fol-

Henry Fonda, Betty Lou Keim, and Allen Case. (Personality Photos)

lowed, and then there was more stage work in 1949's *Texas Li'l Darlin'*, 1953's *The Remarkable Mr. Pennypacker*, and 1955's *A Roomful of Roses*. This background in the theater was something she shared in common with both Henry Fonda and Allen Case, and she said they enjoyed sharing stories about their work in the theatre while on set for *The Deputy*.

Her first television work came in guest shots as the *Armstrong Circle Theatre* program in 1950 and 1951. Her first role in a weekly series was in the summer replacement series *My Son Jeep*, which ran for eleven episodes in the summer of 1953; Keim played Peggy Allison, the daughter of Dr. Robert Allison, in this situation comedy based on the radio series. Guest spots in several other series followed, including the anthologies *Robert Montgomery Presents* and *General Electric Theater.*

Keim received fine notices in her ongoing theatre, television and film career—and had worked with James Cagney (*These Wilder Years*), Ginger Rogers (*Teenage Rebel*), and Frank Sinatra and Dean Martin (*Some Came Running*) in the process. In these years she was often cast as a rebellious youth. At one point in her career, she was under contract to both Twentieth Century-Fox and MGM at the same time.

Her casting in *The Deputy* helped to generate a lot of the series' high-profile before it ever aired, and she always had the best things to say about working with Henry Fonda and Allen Case.

However, in early February, 1960, it was announced that both Betty Lou Keim and Wallace Ford would be written out of the series by April. [116] But Fran McCord, at least, was not being written out of the show based on a format change that the producers were seeking—Keim left the series on her own. She had had a nasty exchange on the set one day with one of the directors, Sidney Lanfield, during which Lanfield had been verbally abusive and Keim told him off. [117]

She decided to leave the series and show business entirely, for that matter, turning down two proposed series leads in 1961 to stay with her husband, actor Warren Berlinger, who was then appearing on Broadway in *Come Blow Your Horn*. [118]

Betty Lou Keim never looked back. The couple happily raised four children and enjoyed eight grandchildren. She died January 27, 2010, after a battle with lung cancer. She was 71. [119]

The loss of the Fran McCord character drastically changed the dynamic of the program from the way it had originally been set forth. The family structure, symbolized by the McCords, was lost, and the series instead shifted focus to Simon, Clay, and "Sarge," the character brought in as Clay's friend during the second season. The loss of the series' only continuing female character meant that perspective was lost, along with the dynamic between brother and sister, between the family and Simon, and between the family and Marshal Herk Lamson. In many ways the McCords were the only family Simon ever had, but *The Deputy* became a male-dominated series and lost that uniqueness once the format changed.

The series also lost the performances of Betty Lou Keim, who had portrayed Fran McCord as a kind, considerate, and intelligent woman, willing to take risks and take a stand to protect her family and her community. She brought a lot to the series and most certainly would have been prominently featured had she continued in the series.

Fran McCord was Clay's seventeen-year-old sister Fran, who was worried constantly about Clay's safety, especially when Simon Fry was in town. Fran had what was described as "an unspoken school-girl crush" [120] on Simon, and knew that just as she might have given in to him, so could her brother. Her defense, as detailed in the Writer's Presentation, was "sometimes a seeming hostility she doesn't feel ... and the perceptive Simon knows it." This is what the audience sees at the close of "The Return of Simon Fry," when Fran pretends that she's not happy that Simon is alive and wasn't killed in a horse and buggy accident.

More to the point was a conversation between Simon and Fran in one of the earliest episodes, "Focus of Doom," written by Sidney Michaels, based on a story idea from producer Michel Kraike. In this episode Simon has sent Herk Lamson on "vacation" because an unknown assassin has killed three marshals in the territory. Simon also refuses to ask Clay to put the deputy's badge on, or tell him why; this angers Clay because he thinks Simon has fired Herk without cause. In reality, Simon is setting himself up to be the only target for the killer. Upset that Simon and Clay are arguing, Fran asks Simon to please tell her what's really wrong. Simon does, telling her, "Miss Fran, honey, I'm going to talk to you as if you was twice seventeen." Fran says, "You're the bravest man I've ever known." [121]

Fran was mature beyond her years, made so by circumstance— the deaths of her father and mother while she was so young. But she often busied herself in the McCord General Store, looking after both of her brothers and becoming involved not only in the family business but in the affairs of her customers. [122] In "Land Greed," broadcast December 12, 1959, she expressed concern to Clay about the selling of rifles to a customer because she was afraid the rifles would be used against a widow whose land is coveted.

Although they appeared in the last episode of the first season, "Ma Mack," broadcast out of sequence, the characters of Fran McCord and Herk Lamson were officially written out of the series with the episode "The Truly Yours," in which the McCord store is burned by outlaws, and Clay picks up the deputy's badge permanently—another big change in the format.

WALLACE FORD as Herk Lamson

"Wally" Ford was one of the old hands of Hollywood when he was cast as the aging marshal of Silver City, Herk Lamson. In his long career in Hollywood and on Broadway, Ford appeared in well over one hundred films and dozens of television series episodes, playing cowboys and mayors, friends and neighbors, heroes and villains. He and Henry Fonda were friends and had acted together in the 1959 western *Warlock* before Ford was cast in *The Deputy*.

Well-liked in the film community and known for keeping things light on the set, Ford debuted as an actor in 1919 on the stage and enjoyed a long and successful career until he died of heart disease on June 11, 1966. When the character of Herk Lamson was written out of the series in the second half of the first season, Ford simply went on working, for as long as his health permitted. Almost immediately, he was cast in a 1960 NBC pilot for a television series which didn't sell, "Three Wishes," though the pilot did eventually aired on CBS in 1963. His last film, 1965's *A Patch of Blue*, starring Sidney Poitier, was still in general release when he died.

"A wonderful guy, a fun guy," Read Morgan recalled. The two actors worked together on the first season episode "Powder Keg." Morgan played Vince, a resident of Silver City deputized by Lamson. "He had a tremendous body of work and a million stories," Morgan said. [123]

Ford's real life was like the plot of one of his films. He never attended school, lived the life of a hobo when he was young, and didn't meet his mother until he was 38 years old.

Wallace Ford and Henry Fonda share a laugh behind the scenes.

Ford was born Samuel Jones Grundy on February 12, 1898, in Batton, England. He survived a childhood that saw him live in seventeen different foster homes after he somehow became separated from his parents. At age 11, and now having lived in Canada for several years, he ran away and joined a vaudeville act, the Winnepeg Kiddies, and stayed with that group until 1914, performing in dance halls as well as vaudeville venues. His stage name was adopted from a hobo. Service in World War I at Fort Riley, Kansas, preceded his stage appearance in Chicago in Booth Tarkington's *Seventeen* in 1919.

For all of the tumult of these early years, Ford and his wife enjoyed one of the longest running marriages in Hollywood. He and actress Martha Haworth were married on November 27, 1922, welcomed a daughter five years later, and were married for the rest of their lives.

His Broadway plays included *Abraham Lincoln* and *Gypsy* and his first film appearance (except for two shorts at Warner Brothers) was in the Joan Crawford vehicle *Possessed* (1931). He signed with MGM in 1932.

Ford's meeting with his mother finally came in 1937, after a long search in England. He found his mother and her husband living in a trailer. While they didn't want to move to America, they did allow him to buy them a cottage in Manchester.

It's been argued that of his many films, Ford's best were his eight *film noirs*—*Shadow of a Doubt* (1943), *Black Angel* (1946), *Crack-Up* (1946), *Dead Reckoning* (1947), *T- Men* (1948), *The Set-Up* (1949), *The Breaking Point* (1950), and *He Ran All the Way* (1951). [124]

Ford's character on *The Deputy* was in line with the character parts he'd been playing in westerns since 1950, including 1959's *Warlock* with Fonda and Richard Widmark. In the film Ford plays a judge in the town that hires a gunfighter to help keep the peace.

Herk Lamson was the marshal of Silver City, but old for the job (Herk was in his mid-fifties). Simon Fry knew this, but kept Herk on because he respected the lawman Lamson once was, and because when the chips were down Herk could still be counted on to do his best. However, there were also times when Herk had to count on Clay McCord for help. Clay was more willing to help Herk than he was to help Simon Fry, because the two had a grandfather-grandson relationship. Herk was part of the McCord family, and the McCords looked out for him and protected him in every way possible— and tried to do so without letting Herk know they were doing it. Simon Fry was no different; as in "Focus of Doom," when Fry tells Herk to go on vacation rather than have him stay in Silver City while an assassin is targeting marshals.

Conceptually, the Herk Lamson character was probably the weakest link in *The Deputy*. The idea that a frontier town could permit an ineffectual marshal to stay in office was hard to swallow. Even Micah Torrance, the marshal of North Fork on *The Rifleman*, while needing constant help from series hero Lucas McCain, had many scenes in various episodes where he would help McCain solve the mystery at hand. In some episodes, he was even able to keep McCain on the true path by imparting wisdom based on his years of experience.

Herk Lamson, on the other hand, didn't have many of these opportunities. While in episodes such as "Lawman's Blood" (February 6, 1960) he is seen ably leading a posse, and in "The Two Faces of Bob Claxton" he helps fight off the Claxton gang, in too many other episodes it simply isn't believable that he is the respected citizen of Silver City that he is described as in the series Writer's Presentation. [125] In "Focus of Doom," Clay throws flour in his face and ties him to a chair to prevent Herk from putting his life in danger.

Herk was designed to serve as a grandfather figure to the Mc-Cords, but there weren't enough scenes fleshing this idea out, even though fans had reacted positively to the family angle on the program. Herk's fate as a character was perhaps sealed in the very first episode when Fry refers to him in a piece of voice-over narration as "a good man, but an old man." [126] Either way, the character had less to do when Betty Lou Keim left the series; absent the conflict between brother and sister over Clay's deputy duties, there really was no reason to keep Herk Lamson around, dramatically speaking—Clay was the deputy.

The series might have put Wallace Ford's fine talent as a character actor to better use as a retired marshal, or city mayor or circuit judge, dispensing sage advice to the McCords and providing the series with some comic relief, rather than as an ineffective marshal who needs watching over from the local storekeeper. The idea that Herk Lamson could lead by example simply didn't play.

READ MORGAN as Sergeant Hapgood Tasker

The second season of *The Deputy* opened with a strong episode titled "The Deadly Breed," about Simon trying to rescue the daughter of a woman he once cared for from the clutches of a con man. The season was off to a good start, but it was the second episode which introduced a major new character and gave the series a new direction.

In the absence of Fran and Herk in the later episodes of the first season, various townspeople had been used to bring Clay news and to interact with him, especially the character of Jose (Vito Scotti), who appeared in six episodes. But it was decided that a permanent, recurring character was needed to fill the role of sidekick.

In "Meet Sergeant Tasker," broadcast October 1, 1960, actor Read Morgan was introduced as Hapgood Tasker, the cavalry sergeant assigned to Silver City as a supply officer who is immediately victimized

The season two cast: Henry Fonda, Read Morgan,
and Allen Case. (Photo courtesy of Read Morgan)

by a trio of thieves. "The producer told me later that they wanted to put in a character that was like a young Victor McLaglen," Morgan said. [127]

Morgan at the time was under contract to MCA, a thirteen-week contract at $350 a week, with ten weeks guaranteed. "I really didn't want to do the series because being under contract I had a chance to play different parts because of all the shows they were doing. Revue Studios at the time had *Wagon Train, Tales of Wells Fargo,* and *Laramie* and on and on. It was like being in a stock company.

"In those days if they paid you they used you, so it gave you the chance to do a lot of things that you wouldn't normally get a chance to do." [128]

When MCA told Morgan it was either do the series or cancel his contract, he did the series. Morgan called working on the show with Henry Fonda and Allen Case "a joy," and said he learned a lot working with Fonda, especially the idea that an actor came to work prepared. "When you come on that set, wipe your shoes, leave your problems at home, and do the work. He was a task master at that. I was so fortunate to have him early in my career because it's one of those things where you learn great discipline." [129]

Morgan was joining a television series that had already been on the air for a year, and knew what he was up against. "When you come into a series that has been on the air for a year with two stars, one of whom has the stature of Fonda, you've got to allow time for character development," he said that November. "But people have started to recognize me, even without the patch." [130]

"Sarge" Tasker, described as "big, good- natured, and head strong," wore an eye patch because his right eye had been picked. Tasker thus became the latest in a growing line of characters in television westerns living with a physical ailment, be it a limp (Chester in *Gunsmoke*) or a ruined arm (*Tate*). "A lot of people have suggested that I poke a hole in the patch," Morgan said at the time. "But I figured I should play it straight. Besides, if you're going to play the part of someone with a disability, do it right." [131]

Read Morgan enjoyed a long career as a character actor in Hollywood, playing a lot of roles suited to his physique, honed through proper eating and exercise. Morgan was featured in many magazine photo spreads. "I never turned down anything unless I was working on something else," he said. [132]

Morgan was born on January 30, 1931, in Chicago, and spent a couple of years as a basketball star and undergraduate at the University of Kentucky before embarking on his career as an actor. His physique brought him work in tough, masculine roles such as a sheriff, a detective, or muscle, in dozens and dozens of television episodes— twelve episodes of *Gunsmoke* alone—from an appearance in *The US Steel Hour* in 1956 to *Paradise* in 1990. He even appeared on one of the earliest episodes of *The Deputy* in 1959, "Powder Keg," when he was under a work contract with MCA/Revue. His last appearance was in a western film, the Richard Donner-Mel Gibson remake of *Maverick*, in 1994. "I'm at Jodie Foster's table," Morgan said. [133]

So what was it that viewers of *The Deputy* got when they tuned in for season number two? The format had permanently changed about three-quarters of the way through the first season, of course, and as year two got underway Clay McCord was settled in as deputy marshal of Silver City. The humorous interplay between Simon and the McCords that had dominated most of the first year—Simon trying to convince Clay to put on the badge—was largely gone. Now much of the interaction between Simon and Clay was a matter of philosophy—two different ideas about law enforcement. Simon remained the steadfast law enforcement officer with no patience for criminals, while Clay often thought there might be other ways to resolve a situation.

The character of Simon Fry lost some of the twinkle in his eye that had so attracted Fonda to the role in the first place, the humor that Roland Kibbee and Norman Lear had given the character in the pilot episode. It was the humor which had caught the appreciative eye of so many television reviewers in 1959. It wasn't so much that Simon had lost all of the chicanery he had started with—he was still using it to help Clay see things a different way—but by the time the second season rolled around, Simon was Clay's boss, a different situation entirely from where the series had started. Simon no longer needed to trick Clay into law enforcement work. Henry Fonda's cameos in the second season have a more serious tone to them than his cameos in the first season, when he was often seen smiling and nudging the Mc-Cords into one situation or another.

Also, Allen Case as Clay had a little less to play in the second season than he had in the first, in terms of character insights. In the first season, Clay interacted with Simon, his sister, and Herk, the grandfather figure. There were a lot of opportunities to play off different characters, domestic situations, and actors.

In the second season, the characters of Clay McCord and Sarge Tasker were used together in a fashion similar to the old Hollywood buddy genre in that they always had each other's backs. In that sense, Clay was more of the traditional television western lawman in the second season than he had been in the first; he was a stalwart champion of law and order in Silver City, to be certain. However, without the family concerns of serving as a surrogate father to Brandy and big brother to Fran, the character had a different focus.

This is not to suggest that the second season episodes were less than the first-season shows; quite the opposite. The second season contains some very dramatic episodes, and the friendship between Clay and Sarge is strong and appealing for viewers. Clay and Sarge work very well together as a team in the second season's 37 episodes, and had the series gone beyond its two-year run, there would have been plenty of opportunities for even more interplay between the characters.

At the beginning of the series, it had been the casting of a major Hollywood star, the humor, the series' family structure, and the focus on the younger residents of Silver City that had truly separated the series out from the parade of westerns on television at the time. The interaction between Clay and his family was replaced by interaction between Clay and Sarge. Tasker is a fun and lively character and an asset to the series; it's just a shame that audiences never got to see Fran McCord interact with Sergeant Tasker, and that viewers never again got to see Clay interact with his sister.

Sergeant Tasker was a major figure in the 1960- 61 season, appearing in all but three episodes ("The Deadly Breed," "Passage to New Orleans," and "Sally Tornado"). Friend and sounding board to Clay McCord, Tasker was often on patrol with the marshals, helping them maintain order and keep the peace. "Sarge" was a big, lovable character who brought an entirely different dimension to the series than did the recurring characters from the first season. Tasker was used as comic relief when needed, and sometimes acted impulsively, but he was always heroic and willing to make sacrifices for his friends.

In episode after episode he was there for Clay, Simon, and the citizens of Silver City.

In the episode "The Challenger," for example, Tasker agrees to a boxing match to try to help Clay raise $500 to send to Fran in Kansas City. In "Tension Point," Tasker helps Clay search for outlaws, not knowing that they have circled back to Silver City and are holding Simon and a family hostage, and in "Brother in Arms" he helps Clay solve the mystery of a boyhood friend who has returned to Silver City with the reputation of being a killer.

GARY HUNLEY as Brandon McCord

Gary Hunley had a short but highly active career as a child actor, mostly on television. Born in 1948, he first appeared in a 1956 episode of *Dragnet* called "The Big No Suicide" and worked steadily in film and television for the next six years. His final credit was an unsold pilot for a television series called "You're Only Young Once" that aired on CBS in 1962.

In *The Deputy* Brandon McCord was the eight-year-old brother of Clay and Fran McCord, a "typical boy of the period." He idolized Simon Fry and worshipped his older brother Clay. Fran was a mother-figure to him after their parents died.

Brandon is seen in the earliest episodes of the series. In the pilot, for example, he is plainly in awe of Simon Fry, while in "The Shadow of the Noose" he provides Simon with crucial information about a man slipping a gun to a jailed suspect.

In later episodes of the first season various children are seen and heard from, but the character of Brandon was rarely seen. He is referred to in the second-season episode "The Challenger" as being in Kansas City with Fran McCord.

ADDISON RICHARDS as Doc Landy

The Silver City physician in early episodes had been Doc Miller, but as of the episode "Lawman's Blood," Doc Landy was introduced to help with the medical chores. The two characters traded off for the remainder of the first season until Landy took the spot permanently. Landy was originally played by Willis Bouchy, but for the rest of the series run the character was played by Addison Richards.

Richards had a thirty-year career in Hollywood, with hundreds of appearances in film and television starting in 1933 and lasting until his death in 1964. Born October 20, 1887, Richards graduated from Washington State University and Pomona College, and was a dependable character actor who could be counted upon to know his lines and hit his marks. He played an assortment of mostly respected and upstanding citizens, including doctors, law enforcement officers, and military men throughout his career, with an occasional villain thrown in for good measure. He was a regular on four other television series in addition to his run as Doc Landy on *The Deputy*. He starred in and narrated *Pentagon USA* (1953), a series about US Army criminal investigators; appeared as a wealthy rancher on *Cimarron City* (1958), a Western with George Montgomery; as Doc Gamble on *Fibber McGee and Molly* (1959); and as a judge on the daytime soap opera *Ben Jerrod* (1963). He died on March 22, 1964.

Like many other frontier doctors on television, Doc Landy was an older, sometimes irascible doctor counted upon to pull bullets out of marshals and outlaws alike. Landy by his own reckoning was the only doctor around for two hundred miles ("The Choice") and as such he was indispensable to hundreds of people. He was seen to best advantage in the episodes "The Choice," in which Landy took an ex-convict (played by Vince Edwards) under his wing and taught him medicine, and "Day of Fear," in which Simon must quarantine the town because of a suspected smallpox outbreak.

PHIL TULLY as Charlie

Phil Tully had the kind of blue-collar, working man's career in Hollywood that often goes unheralded when stacked up against the major stars of the day. But Tully was also one of those actors who appeared in scores of television shows and films in small character roles, even bit parts, whenever a producer needed a convincing bartender, desk sergeant, or police officer to stand in the background. His Hollywood career started in 1937 and ran for about thirty years, including appearances in *All the King's Men* and *House of Strangers*.

Tully had one of his longest lasting roles when he appeared in several second-season episodes of *The Deputy* as Charlie, the bartender at the saloon in Silver City, which was located directly across the street from the marshal's office. He dispensed drinks, gossip, and advice to Simon, Clay, and Sarge, not to mention the outlaws and tinhorns coming through the town.

VITO SCOTTI as Jose

When Wallace Ford and Betty Lou Keim were no longer regulars on the series, the producers quickly realized they were going to need someone for Clay to interact with on a daily basis—someone he could trust to bring him news of the town, gossip, and warnings about possible dangers. With Simon Fry only a part-time character, especially in the first season, Clay had no one left to interact with on a regular basis.

The problem was addressed for the remainder of the first season with the addition of the character of Jose, a local townsman in Silver City who performed all of these needed dramatic devices. Jose was played by Vito Scotti, who had a long and successful career as a character actor, especially in ethnic roles.

Born January 26, 1918, Scotti began his Hollywood career in 1949 and worked steadily until his death on June 5, 1996. Along the way, he played heroes and heavies, worked in dramas and comedies, and graced every production he was in with a solid performance. Films fans remember him for his roles in films such as *How Sweet It Is!* and *The Godfather*, but he perhaps left his biggest mark on television, where he moved easily from one television guest appearance to the next with an amazing range. While situation comedy fans recall his two turns as Dr. Boris Balinkoff on *Gilligan's Island*, Western fans remember his chilling performance as a crazed Mexican bandit in a two-part episode of *The Rifleman*, "Waste," written by actor Robert Culp.

NORMAN LEAR AND ROLAND KIBBEE

Roland Kibbee and Norman Lear had worked together on *The Tennessee Ernie Ford Show* as writers, and when they started to talk about writing a television western, both wanted to add more humor into the characterizations than what was seen in other television westerns of the period. "We both saw life through the end of the telescope that finds the humor in anything," Lear said. "We used to talk about the foolishness of the human condition, and we always understood that, writing together." [134]

Norman Lear, later to become a dominating force in television and American culture through the creation and development of series such as *All in the Family, Maude,* and *Good Times,* always credited Kibbee with influencing him as a writer.

"Roland Kibbee was a great, lovely writer," Lear said. "And one of the great experiences of my life was knowing him, working with him." [135]

Kibbee (1914- 1984), a one-time stage actor, began his writing career in Los Angeles radio in 1931, and later wrote during the halcyon days of network radio in America, writing comedy for Fred Allen, for whom he was a favorite, Groucho Marx, and Fanny Brice, among others. He was educated at Los Angeles City College and served as a pilot in World War II. After the war, he turned to screenwriting, working on films such as *A Night in Casablanca* and *Angel on My Shoulder* (both 1946). Later, he wrote screenplays for many films, including *Vera Cruz* and *The Crimson Pirate.*

Kibbee's greatest success came on television, however. It was on the small screen where he best displayed his versatility and enormous creative skills as a writer, producer, and creator.

Kibbee not only created *The Deputy* for Henry Fonda, but he also helped to create *The Tennessee Ernie Ford Show* format, and worked on that series as head writer. He created a situation comedy for Bob Cummings in 1961, and the successful 1968-70 adventure series *It Takes a Thief* starring Robert Wagner. Kibbee wrote for many series, including *The Bob Cummings Show;* the first *The Bob Newhart Show* (sharing in the Peabody Award won by that series); *Columbo* with Peter Falk; and the outstanding 1970s comedy *Barney Miller,* for which he won an Emmy (he had an Emmy during his *Columbo* days, as well). As a producer, Kibbee's work is evident in numerous television series, including *Columbo, McCoy, Madigan,* and *Barney Miller,* among others.

Kibbee once said he became a producer as well as a writer because "a producer in TV controls the material and exerts a large measure of influence." But even as a show runner, Kibbee considered himself a writer. [136]

"Having written screenplays," Norman Lear said of Kibbee's work, "he had a sense of form, which applied to the briefest sketch as well as to the longest teleplay or screenplay.

"And I learned as much as I've learned from anybody, far more in a practical way, from Roland Kibbee." [137]

Writer-producer Norman Lear would help Kibbee create *The Deputy* and go on to a pioneering career in television. The importance of his career in television history cannot be overstated. His work on many series, not only *All in the Family* and *Maude,* but also *Sanford and Son, The Jeffersons, One Day at a Time, Good Times,* and *Mary Hartman, Mary Hartman,* makes him one of the most influential people in television history.

Lear was born on July 27, 1922, in New Haven, Connecticut, and was educated at Emerson College in Boston. He entered the entertainment industry after service in World War II. His early television work included writing for Martin & Lewis, Martha Raye, and George Gobel, before meeting Roland Kibbee on *The Tennessee Ernie Ford Show.*

In 1959, Lear formed a business and production partnership with director-producer Bud Yorkin that eventually led to the production of television specials and feature films.

Lear's association with Fonda didn't end with the creation of *The Deputy*. In 1962, Fonda hosted a Yorkin-Lear television special called *Henry Fonda and the Family*. "It was a wonderful show," Lear said. "It examined, off the Census, the status of the American family."

Fonda later hosted a retrospective of Lear's *All in the Family* series in 1974, and Lear also purchased a home from actor-director Paul Henreid that had originally been built for Fonda.

Lear's historic television series, starting with *All in the Family* in 1971, were known as much for their sensitivity toward people and issues as they were for the controversial topics they often addressed; the programs never shied away from the important issues of the day. Indeed, his television series thrived on presenting those issues, talking about them, and thinking about them, whether the issue was racism, bigotry, anti-Semitism, or any other issue facing the country.

President Bill Clinton awarded Lear the National Medal of Art in 1999, saying, he "has held a mirror up to American society and changed the way we look at it."

The awards list is long and plentiful, including Emmy Awards, a Peabody Award, an Oscar nomination for best screenplay, and numerous lifetime achievement awards. His impact on American television is incalculable.

In 2000, The Lear Center at the USC Annenberg School for Communication and Journalism was named for him following his gift of financial support; the Center studies "the social, political, economic, and cultural impact of entertainment on the world." [138] His ongoing work in various media in the 21st century can be seen at normanlear.com.

The Deputy became the first network television series to carry the words "created by" and "Norman Lear" in the end credits. "It was the first drama or sitcom where there was a film credit [for me]," Lear said, "Where something might be repeated through the years, as *The Deputy* was." [139]

Not that Lear ever saw huge earnings from his co-creation. "For years and years afterwards, I tried everything I knew how to find out why they're telling me they haven't made another nickel. I never got a nickel."

The creation of *The Deputy* resulted from the collaboration between these two enormously talented and creative men. Once the series went into production, as is often the case in television, the series itself was in the hands of other talents. Roland Kibbee was credited with an on-screen writing credit on three other episodes beyond the pilot, and Norman Lear none. However, their unique contribution to the western genre on television can still be found in the series pilot, "Badge for a Day," the decidedly non- western Western (see chapter four).

WILLIAM FRYE AND MICHEL KRAIKE

The Deputy was produced by Henry Fonda's Top Gun Company through Revue Productions, what was then the television division of the Music Corporation of America, better known as the talent agency MCA. Revue was incorporated in 1950.

MCA made arrangements for production space at the old Republic Studios on Radford Avenue in North Hollywood to house Revue, and started to produce dozens of television series, including many series for MCA's celebrity clients. In 1959, MCA purchased the Universal Pictures lot in Universal City on Lankershim Boulevard and renamed it Revue Studios. [140]

The Universal lot in those years was very different. Author Robert Bloch, who went to work on the lot in 1959 for the Alfred Hitchcock series, said later, "Those who've visited the studio in recent years would be completely lost if a time machine transported them back through the gates of 1959.

"There were no tours then, and no traffic problems. After proper identification one simply drove in and found a convenient parking place.

"Just left of the studio entrance was the rambling old commissary where—in defiance of natural law—the stars did come out at noon." [141]

The quality of the series produced by Revue varied greatly, and in its history Revue "gained a reputation for quantity at the expense of quality." [142] The criticism was that Revue produced an astonishingly large amount of product, and that a lot of it was run-of-the-mill, by-the-numbers product, even as Revue built itself into one of the most successful producers of film for television at that time, along with Desilu, Four Star, and Screen Gems.

Still, some of the series produced by MCA/Revue are among the best remembered of the day—programs like *Alfred Hitchcock Presents, M Squad, General Electric Theatre, Wagon Train,* and even *Leave it to Beaver.* The Hitchcock series, in particular, was consistently well-written, produced, and acted, and it ran for ten years in both half- hour and hour-long formats. Other series included *The Restless Gun,* starring John Payne and based on James Stewart's *The Six Shooter* radio series, *Biff Baker, USA, Tales of Wells Fargo* and *State Trooper.* The quality did vary greatly, series to series.

General Electric Theater was another high-quality program, and more than any other series, it capitalized on the relationships to MCA clients, booking an impressive list of Hollywood stars, season after season, episode after episode. James Stewart took two *Six Shooter* scripts he owned and starred in them for the series, and Alan Ladd made his only three television dramatic appearances on *General Electric Theater*.

The producer most closely associated with the GE series was William Frye, who started as a talent agent but moved into series production in network radio on series such as *Tales of the Texas Rangers* and *Yours Truly, Johnny Dollar*. On television, he produced series such as *Halls of Ivy, The Bob Cummings Show, Johnny Staccato*, and episodes of anthology programs like *Four Star Playhouse, Startime* and *Suspicion*. Later, Frye was tabbed to produce a promising series that had gotten off to a troubled start, *Thriller*, with Boris Karloff, and is credited with saving the program. By the time he got to *The Deputy* in 1959, Frye was a respected and well-liked producer. Donald S. Sanford, who worked with Frye on *Thriller*, said Frye was "excellent at casting, knew the art of storytelling." [143]

On *The Deputy*, Frye produced the pilot film, and his hand is very evident in it. Silver City is impressively staged in "Badge for a Day" and looks like a bustling frontier community. But as the series went into full episodic production, Frye served as executive producer, leaving the day-to-day producing chores to Michael Kraike, also billed as Michel Kraike.

Kraike had been producing films in Hollywood since 1943, most notably the Henry Aldrich series, and the film *Criss Cross*. He moved into television series work in the 1950s and produced episodes of *The Ford Television Theatre, The Damon Runyon Theatre* and *The 20ᵗʰ Century-Fox Hour* before being named an administrative executive at Twentieth Century-Fox Television in 1956. He formed his own production company in 1957 to try to develop film and television projects.

In addition to his producing chores for *The Deputy*, Kraike also contributed several scripts to the series.

It was a veteran team that came together to produce *The Deputy* at Revue, no doubt contributing to the fact that the series looked as good as it did, despite the frenetic pace of production.

Of course, it was Fonda's company producing the series, and his influence was especially evident in the casting. "They always had good people," Read Morgan said. "Fonda oversaw the casting." [144]

Director David Butler told a funny story about the casting process for "The Choice," which aired during the second season on June 25, 1960. "One day a young man came and stood in my box at the track, watching the race. One of the horses was about fifth, and then it started to move up. This fellow yelled and screamed, and the horse won. Then he grabbed me around the neck and shouted, 'I had it! I had it!' and ran out of my box.

"The next day I was doing a picture with Henry Fonda. We were trying to get a cast together. They brought in various people to read. One of them was the same fellow who had been in the box the day before. He read the scene, and he read it better than any of the others. I recommended that he get the part. He was Vince Edwards." [145] Edwards said later it was his part in this episode which landed him his signature role as Ben Casey on the medical series of the same name.

Not only was the casting of the principals first-rate, but the guest stars shone. First-season guest stars included Marie Windsor, Whitney Blake, Robert J. Wilkie, Denver Pyle, Clu Gulager, Martha Hyer, Tom Laughlin, Vivian Vance, Lillian Bronson, and Charles McGraw. Second-season guest stars included James Franciscus, Richard Crenna, Fay Spain, Denny Miller, Lon Chaney, Jr., Norma Crane, Whit Bissell, Johnny Cash, Vince Edwards, and Mary Tyler Moore. Several of the guest stars who appeared during the two-year run of the series had also appeared with Fonda in *Warlock* in 1959.

JACK MARSHALL, BOB BAIN AND HOWARD ROBERTS

Composer Jack Marshall (1921- 1973) was hired to compose the music score for *The Deputy* in 1959 following his work in several motion pictures, including *The Giant Gila Monster* that year. Before his death in 1973, Marshall would score other television series from various genres. His credits run from westerns (*Laredo*) to comedy (*The Debbie Reynolds Show*) to police drama (*The Investigators.*) He's well remembered today for his theme to the television series T*he Munsters*.

During the run of *The Deputy,* Marshall released his third album for Capitol Records, called *The Marshall Swings* (the other two up to that time were *18th Century Jazz* and *Soundsville*). [146]

For *The Deputy,* Marshall featured the harmonica and the jazz guitar, both of which he loved. [147] Marshall used five guitars as the main sound of the orchestra. Howard Roberts and Bob Bain were among the guitarists, and Roberts improvised in scenes in many different episodes. Multiple guitars were used; the use of the jazz guitar in a television series was unique in 1959 and the work gave the series a distinctive sound. [148]

Roberts was a prolific guitarist; his work, he once estimated, could be heard on more than two thousand records. On television, his guitar work could be heard on *I Love Lucy, Gilligan's Island, Get Smart,* and *The Addams Family,* but perhaps his most memorable television work was the opening notes of *The Twilight Zone* and the bluegrass heard in the theme from *The Beverly Hillbillies.*

Roberts performed as a backup musician for Frank Sinatra, Elvis Presley, Ray Charles, and many others. He founded the Guitar Institute of Technology in Hollywood in 1977; it later became The Musicians Institute.

Roberts died in a Seattle Hospital of prostate cancer in 1992.

Bob Bain was born in Chicago on January 26, 1924, and his career in film and television began with background guitar work on *The Adventures of Ozzie and Harriet* television series in 1952, but by that time he had been a musician for many, many years, in bands, touring nightclubs, and had played with Tommy Dorsey.

His work in series television ranged from *Gunsmoke* to *Peter Gunn* and *Bonanza*. He worked for more than twenty years in the guitar chair as part of "The Tonight Show Band" on *The Tonight Show Starring Johnny Carson*. In films, he worked in a variety of genres, including music for *Doctor Dolittle*, *Rosemary's Baby*, *Blazing Saddles*, and *Escape from the Planet of the Apes*, to name just a few. Bain worked on hundreds of films and television programs.

CHAPTER FOUR

Not *The Tin Star*

"That was the Arizona Territory in 1880, and I was its Chief Marshal."

— Marshal Simon Fry

T he television Western wave of the 1950s and early 1960s on which *The Deputy* rode did not just appear out of nowhere; it evolved from the Western in other forms of popular culture, including novels, magazines, films, and radio. The Western, as Malachi Topping pointed out, "goes deep into American historical roots." [149]

The rise of the Western as a literary form has been traced to the novels of James Fenimore Cooper, whose work was used as model for countless other writers and eventually the themes were adopted by filmmakers, as well.

Cooper's Leatherstocking Tales, from 1823- 1841, and his hero, Natty Bumppo, were imitated almost endlessly. The popularized ideas of the western hero, the wilderness setting, and adventure have been providing many Westerns with their starting point ever since. These stories spoke of the individual and the encroachment of society.

The 1885 publication of "A Texas Cowboy," Charles Siringo's account of his life as a teenage cowboy, captured all the adventure and mythos that Americans would come to associate with the Wild West and what eventually they would want in their Westerns.

The dime novelists pushed the Western out to the masses, and Owen Wister's *The Virginian* (1902) provided the modern Western hero and that hero's relationship with other characters. For proof of the novel's impact on the filmed Western one need look no further than at the number of times it had been filmed—1914, 1923, 1929, and 1946—long before the television western was born.

The novels of authors Zane Grey and Max Brand (Frederick Faust) made the Western even more popular, and, much later, writers such as Luke Short (Frederick Glidden), Louis L'Amour and Ernest Haycox, among many others, enhanced its legitimacy and ensured its popularity.

The motion picture Western was born just a year after *The Virginian* with the release of *The Great Train Robbery*, giving the genre its visual style and shape. The vistas seen in the Western not only help tell the story, with the hero often battling the very land and nature he's fighting to save, but the grandeur of the Western setting was a large part of the appeal for audiences.

The roots of the Western on film, then, are here, at the turn of the century. John G. Cawelti said that it was in the publication of *The Virginian* and the release of *The Great Train Robbery* that "the modern western was born, synthesizing some of the adventurous and mythical qualities of the dime novels with more sophisticated and adult treatments of history, setting, and character." [150]

There were many fine Westerns filmed before 1939, *The Big Trail* (1930) and *The Plainsman* (1936) among them, but the true Golden

Age of the A List Western motion picture began in 1939 with the release of four films: director John Ford's *Stagecoach,* George Marshall's
Destry Rides Again, Ford's *Drums Along the Mohawk,* and Cecil B.
DeMille's *Union Pacific;* from that point forward the major Westerns
didn't stop coming for a quarter-century, producing not only Hollywood stars such as Joel McCrea and Randolph Scott, but one of the
country's foremost figures in popular culture: John Wayne.

The Western was introduced to even larger mass audiences
through electronic communications starting in 1930 on radio with
the premiere of the *Death Valley Days* anthology series, followed by
The Lone Ranger in 1933, an immensely popular series about a Texas
Ranger who survives an ambush and devotes his life to helping others in jeopardy. While the Western was never the dominant genre
on radio that it would be on television, writers, producers, and actors of radio produced several outstanding and well-regarded series,
including *Gunsmoke* (1952), focusing on U.S. Marshal Matt Dillon
and the residents of Dodge City, Kansas in the 1870s; *The Six Shooter*
(1953), with James Stewart as an amiable cowboy drifting in and out
of other people's problems; and *Frontier Gentleman* (1958), the tales
of a reporter for a London newspaper wandering in the western ter-
ritories. These series featured adult heroes in morality plays, as good
confronted evil in its many forms in the West (bandits and outlaws,
con men, mercenaries), week after week.

The Western was part of television from the beginning of the medium, first as national children's programs and live afternoon children's
programs produced on local stations. The adult Western cycle started
in 1952 with the television version of *Death Valley Days* and was shot
into the stratosphere of popularity with the premieres of *The Life and*

Legend of Wyatt Earp, Cheyenne, Frontier, and the television version of *Gunsmoke,* all in 1955. (Nothing, however, ever quite matched the Davy Crockett phenomenon starting in December 1954, with the premiere of the first Crocket episode on the Disney television program on ABC. It's been estimated that in the first seven to eight months of the "Crockett Craze" in 1955, more than $300 million worth of merchandise was sold. That's more than two billion dollars in 2001 dollars.) [151]

There's no doubt that the television Western took its characters, plots, and themes from its predecessors in literature and film; its look from Western films; and its lessons in series building and reaching a mass audience from network radio.

The television western was different from its film counterpart, though, in that its focus was not on the "wide open spaces" of the big screen, the large canvas of visuals portraying the vastness of the West. Because of budgetary constraints, and the number of episodes to be produced, television westerns tended to focus on human problems, rather than the sense of physical place. [152]

The television Western was a simple, straight-forward morality tale played out in short individual episodes. The television genre would utilize familiar plots such as those involving wagon trains, ranchers, lawmen, outlaws, and the Native American, and was "likely to draw its conflicts from the range of human drama found across the spectrum of ancient myths up to and including contemporary issues." [153]

By the time *The Deputy* went into production in early 1959, the Western had been a major part of popular culture for decades. The staggering challenge for the program's writers, actors, and producers, then, was to use what was familiar and attractive to audiences, the Western formula, while at the same time giving the series its own creative twist. Given the vast numbers of Westerns already on network television, this was no easy task. The choice the creative team made was not to root the series in props (special pistols, rifles), gimmicks (white hats and horses), or fictionalized history, but instead in

Henry Fonda as Simon Fry, 1959. (Photofest)

its characters. It wasn't that the series didn't have action and adventure—it did-- but it added youth, family, and humor to the mix.

When Roland Kibbee and Norman Lear first presented their pilot script, "Badge for a Day," for the series that would eventually be called *The Deputy*, they were facing a crowded field of westerns on television. The western genre dominated television at the start of the 1959-60 network season. The previous season, there had been a total of twenty-five westerns on the air; for the 1959- 1960 season, this total would grow to thirty westerns in prime time on the three networks. (The television western craze would die quickly when the end did come, however. The number of new and remaining Westerns on television would drop to a mere handful by the start of the 1963- 64 season, never to return to its earlier prominence.)

Of the thirty westerns on air in 1959-1960, thirteen were new shows and seventeen were holdovers from the previous season, including powerhouses such as *Gunsmoke* and *Maverick*. The new programs included *Bonanza, Wichita Town, Laramie,* and *The Rebel*. The westerns came in all shapes and sizes, and the characters involved were in all sorts of occupations ranging from cowboys to sheriffs, ranchers to lawmen, and newspapermen to bounty hunters.

"Badge for a Day" told the story of how Simon Fry, chief marshal of the Arizona territory in 1880, maneuvered storekeeper Clay McCord into helping him bust up the Ace Gentry gang then running loose in the area around Silver City. That Fry would trick the reluctant McCord into believing that he and Simon were delivering supplies to a nearby community, when in fact they were running those supplies, undercover, to the Gentry gang, immediately set this marshal apart from his peers on television. [155]

As Fonda said himself, he was playing "a grizzled lawman who is not opposed to resorting to a bit of chicanery occasionally as he maintains justice…" [156] In one of the pilot's first scenes, Fry arrests two members of the gang for polluting a stream after one of the men spits in the dry creek bed. When the man protests there's no water in the creek, Fry says, "The law don't say nuthin' about water." [157] Later, Fry makes one of the men talk by pretending to burn the other, out of sight but within earshot, with a spur heated on a lamp.

Eventually, Fry and McCord make their way to the Gentry Gang's camp and after the usual fisticuffs and shots fired, apprehend the outlaws. Clay's sister Fran is none too happy with Simon for tricking her brother into taking part, but Simon points out to her that Clay could have pulled out at any time if he'd really wanted to. Clay tries to give back the deputy's badge Simon gave him, but Simon refuses to take it, telling Clay that "You never know when you might be usin' it again." [158]

"Badge for a Day" was well-received by television writers and critics of the time. "The new Fonda series, *The Deputy*, seems to me to have lively qualities which set it apart from the usual western formula," wrote Cecil Smith in *The Los Angeles Times*. [159] The script was praised for its humor and its characterizations by other writers, pleased to see something a little different from the standard television western. In reviewing the show, columnist Janet Kerns noted the sex appeal of Allen Case, the polish and professionalism of Henry Fonda, and added that "another sterling virtue of this premiere was the script (magnificently written with plenty of humor in the dialogue and solemnity in the plot)." [160]

Not everyone was thrilled with the program. *Broadcasting*, despite calling the show the season's best new western, was certain that the device of Simon tricking Clay into helping him would "get old rather quickly," [161] while *Variety* cited what it called the series' "lack of artistic merit" and called it a "standard hoss opera." The newspaper also wrote that as Fry, "Fonda was an easy-going enforcer of the law, a little dumber than he was wry," and said Betty Lou Keim as Fran McCord "provided more eye appeal than conflict." [162]

Years later, looking back on the career of series co-creator Roland Kibbee, authors Christopher Wicking and Tise Vahimagi would describe *The Deputy* as a "self-consciously non-western," [163] suggesting that the series had the humor of Kibbee's 1954 Western film, *Vera Cruz,* the satirical Gary Cooper-Burt Lancaster vehicle in which two men are involved in a scheme in Mexico to overthrow the emperor.

The humor in *The Deputy* came from the characters. Kibbee and Norman Lear had tried for something different in the pilot and had found it.

The pilot was absolutely not, as some sources claim, [164] an adaptation of Fonda's 1957 film, *The Tin Star.* Fonda did not play the same character in the series that he had played in the film, and nor was the series a spin-off from or continuation of the film. The truth of the matter is that the idea for *The Deputy* came from a surprising source and from a far different place than fans of the television western might expect.

The Tin Star, written by Dudley Nichols from a story by Joel Kane and Barney Slater, and directed by Anthony Mann, starred Fonda as Morgan Hickman, a former lawman-turned-bounty hunter who arrives in a western town looking to collect the bounty on the outlaw he captured and killed. He befriends the town's young sheriff, Ben Owens, played by Anthony Perkins, and schools him on a variety of law enforcement skills and life lessons designed to help the sheriff against the town's criminal element.

Fonda and Case, 1959 (Western TV Photos)

The film was highly praised upon its release, and was nominated for an Oscar for its screenplay and a BAFTA Award as best film. In the years since its initial release, the film has gained even more status as a lean, character-driven western.

Henry Fonda is wonderful in the film, playing Morg Hickman as a deeply melancholy, even sad, man with a hardness and loneliness that is plainly visible in his eyes. The embittered Hickman has seen it all and arrives in town only to collect reward money, but finding instead his salvation.

In *The Tin Star*, Morg Hickman has left the law behind, embittered by the death of his wife and young son. For much of the film he refuses repeated requests from newly- appointed Sheriff Ben Owens to put a badge back on, though in the end he is redeemed not only by a renewed sense of justice embodied by the young sheriff, but also through his growing feelings for a white woman and her young Native-American son.

In *The Deputy*, Simon Fry stands for law and order in the territory. Time and time again we see Fry maintaining the peace. Unlike Morg Hickman, Fry has not left the law behind; in fact, it is his life. The Writer's Presentation for the series described Fry as "dedicated almost mono-maniacally to the principles of justice and law that have out of necessity contemporaneously generated in the West." [166]

The relationship between Hickman and Owens in *The Tin Star* is a mentorship, with the older, wiser, more experienced man tutoring the younger man on the ways of the world. During a shooting lesson, for example, Hickman advises Owens that if he's going to shoot, "shoot to kill." [167] As pointed out in *The BFI Companion to the Western*, "Of all the common motifs in the Western, the scene in which the hero passes on his knowledge of the gun is perhaps that which most obviously binds the genre into a system of patriarchal authority. Usually the recipient is a young boy or youth..." [168] Hickman also counsels the young sheriff on how to approach a man on the street.

While the young-old relationship is again used in *The Deputy*, young Clay McCord is depicted as being on far more equal footing with Simon Fry than Ben Owens was to Morg Hickman in *The Tin Star*. Fry often refers to McCord as the top gun in the territory. Clay, especially in the earliest episodes of the series, is reluctant to use his gun at all, no matter what his expertise. He deplores violence, and wonders what life would be like in Silver City if men didn't carry guns. Even in later episodes, after Clay has taken over as Silver City marshal from Herk Lamson, he resorts to gunplay only as a last resort. Clay battles Fry whenever he feels justified; there is no "stay and teach me" type dialogue between Fry and McCord, as there is between Hickman and Owens at the close of *The Tin Star*.

Finally, Simon Fry is anything but sad and melancholy. Simon is filled with humor and genuine fondness for his friends. He smiles at a good joke, perks up at the sight of a pretty woman (guest Martha Hyer, for example, in the first-season episode "Hang the Law"), and tells Fran McCord she's "getting prettier every day" [169] ("The Two Faces of Bob Claxton").

This is not to say that a series based on Fonda's character of Morgan Hickman would not have made for an interesting series. In fact, the interplay between Fonda, Betsy Palmer, as Nona Mayfield, and Michel Ray, as Kip Mayfield, is one of the strengths of the film and surely would have made for interesting frontier stories on television. Indeed, that series would have had the opportunity to provide further insights into some of the underlying themes of the film, such as intolerance and racial bigotry, as seen through the eyes of the young boy, but that is not the series Fonda signed on for in 1959. (Paramount did try to mount a television version of *The Tin Star* in 1968, developed by *Gunsmoke* creator John Meston and producer Stan Kallis, but the series didn't sell.)

However, if *The Deputy* did not spring from *The Tin Star*, where did the idea come from? The answer is likely to surprise fans of the television western genre.

"[Roland Kibbee] had the idea," Norman Lear said. "He called me and said Henry Fonda was interested in doing a television show, and [he said], 'I'm thinking about a western' and we started to talk about a western.

"We came across the idea of taking the relationship that existed in Ben Hecht's *Front Page*," Lear said, "in which an editor had a star reporter who was threatening to leave and then deciding to leave, hated journalism, he didn't want to be in that rat race anymore."

The Front Page premiered on Broadway in 1928, and was written by Hecht and Charles MacArthur. The play, about the relationship between the editor and his top reporter in Chicago in the 1920s, would be filmed several times, perhaps most famously with Cary Grant and Rosalind Russell as *His Girl Friday*, and remains influential in its frenetic depiction of the world of journalism.

"When the curtain went up," Norman Lear said, "that editor had some years of—every trick in the world to keep that reporter at the newspaper working for him." [170]

Lear and Kibbee took that relationship and turned it into "a sheriff, who had a young assistant sheriff, who was going to hold onto him because the guy was so great." [171]

In "Badge for a Day," the two writers were trying to separate their series out from the many others westerns on network television by adding humor and by focusing on the interplay between Simon Fry and Clay McCord. Their relationship was built on the idea that Fry and McCord were like friendly enemies— just as in *The Front Page*.

Henry Fonda as Simon Fry, defending the
Arizona Territory, 1959. (Western TV Photos)

As stated in the series' Writer's Guide, "A wide gulf of attitudes and outlooks separates the two men, but a sturdy bridge of mutual admiration and regard binds them together." [172]

But there was more to the series concept than that. In "Badge for a Day," there is a remarkable scene in the McCord General Store in which Clay, a gunsmith as well as storekeeper, tells a customer that he won't work on handguns, only rifles, because handguns were "used for killin' people" while rifles were "used for killin' meat." Clay is clearly more than just a typically reluctant sharpshooter—the kind of stock character found in westerns all over television and film-- when he tells the customer, "Ever cross your mind that if nobody ever carried a shootin' iron there wouldn't be no shootin'?" [173]

"Kibbee also had a great sense of what was important in life," Lear said. "He had a great deal of political and social feeling, and his work always reflected it. In that first episode, we had a young deputy who didn't believe in handguns. It had something to say, and that was so typical of Kibbee, and as it later turned out to be, of me." [174]

THE BIBLE

In 1959, nearly every television series had a written series concept of some kind, a blueprint, or series bible, or Writer's Guide. Call it what you will, in the end this blueprint, or road map, pointed the way forward.

The blueprint is the place where writers look for insights into characters, themes, setting, and sample storylines. It is also the place where writers can discover their limits—what a character might or might not do, and what kind stories producers were looking for and not looking for.

The series bible was especially important in the first two or three decades of television, when freelance writers were more prolific than they were later; as television grew older, when much of the writing done for a television series would be done by a more permanent in-house writing staff.

In the case of *The Deputy*, this document was dated May 13, 1959, and was titled "Presentation to Writers of a New Television Series Tentatively Entitled--- 'The Deputy.'"

This Writer's Guide described the format of the series, including its manner of presentation, background, characters, the relationships between the characters, the style of the show, and its boundaries and limits. Like all of these "bibles," it was designed to point writers in the right direction and hopefully leading them to the creation of cost- effective scripts with compelling stories.

In the case of *The Deputy*, as with all television series, some of the episodes were better than others. But no producer sets out to produce poor episodes—it is simply a matter of time, resources, and budgeting. The production of episodic television was then, and is now, as much about the practical application of resources as it is about art or craft.

A PRESENTATION TO WRITERS

From the beginning, *The Deputy* was designed as a half-hour television western series, with six of the episodes starring Henry Fonda and co-starring Allen Case and Wallace Ford. These six episodes would be told from the point of view of Simon Fry, Fonda's character, with Fry often narrating the story. The remaining episodes would concentrate on Allen Case's character, Clay McCord.

In the very first scene of the pilot episode, "Badge for a Day," we hear the first voice-over of Henry Fonda, in all of his quiet but firm authority, revealing exactly where we are and with whom: "That was the Arizona Territory in 1880 and I was its chief marshal." [175]

It would become the series' signature line.

Each episode was to open with "an exciting action or suspenseful teaser" which would lead into the rest of the episode. The idea was to establish jeopardy or motivating action for the principal characters or for guest stars who would impact the regulars. As for Simon Fry, the Writer's Guide said:

> In the teaser or in the scene immediately following, Simon Fry will be introduced against an interesting background, or by a character who will lead us to him in the inception of the story and by its motivating elements; and we will learn of Fry's interest and attitude regarding an event or events to follow. In those episodes where he is not the dominant character, we will learn the reasons why he is unable to attend to the case himself and how either he— or events themselves—inveigle McCord into accepting deputization. [176]

The teaser would take on many forms during the course of the series. In "The Hard Decision," broadcast as the 18th episode of season two on January 18, 1961, the teaser involves outlaws threatening the safety of the principal characters, while in "Focus of Doom," broadcast November 7, 1959, the opening sequence depicted three sheriffs being gunned down. Fry was seen in the scene immediately following the tease galloping across the prairie toward Silver City because he feared Herk Lamson, his marshal there, might be next.

Allen Case as Clay McCord, 1959 (Western TV Photos)

Fry and McCord were the focal point characters from the start of the series; all others were subordinate to them. Indeed, before the end of the first season, other recurring characters were written out of the show, starting with the episode "The Truly Yours," and even more screen time could be devoted to Fry and McCord.

BACKGROUND

The stories seen and heard in "The Deputy" take place in 1880, in the Arizona Territory—more specifically, the Southwest section of the territory bordering along and North Mexico. The cow and mining town called Silver City is the chief locale for the series. The choice of 1880 as the year events in the series took place was keeping with the television westerns of the day, most of which were set in the years between the end of the Civil War and before the turn of the century.

Nor was *The Deputy* unique among western series of the late 1950s and early 1960s in its use of Arizona as the geographic locale. In fact, several did, including *Boots and Saddles, Johnny Ringo, Broken Arrow,* and *Tombstone Territory.* Other series such as *Bat Masterson* and *The Life and Legend of Wyatt Earp* often set episodes in Arizona. The territory was home to a wide range of people—Indian tribes, Civil War veterans from the North and the South, settlers, outlaws—opening up the narrative possibilities.

Arizona was useful to *The Deputy* and these other series as a background because it combined a rugged persona and wide-open spaces with the coming of civilization in places like Silver City. There were mountains, prairie, desert, and open range in which to place narratives, adding to the variety of stories. Simon Fry could often be seen riding across the desert and other rugged backdrops as he narrated the tales of *The Deputy*.

Specific physical settings—the places where action occurred--used in television westerns include the saloon, the sheriff's office, shops, the community street, a ranch, and a local hotel. These physical settings were seen in *The Deputy* in the form of the general store belonging to the McCords, the streets of Silver City, the Silver City marshal's office, the hotel across the street from the marshal's office, and local ranches in and around Silver City (for example, the ranch owned by the Brown family in the episode "The Return of Widow Brown," broadcast April 22, 1961).

As Don Kirkley wrote, "The stores, shops, and offices and the town hotel provided locales for confrontation with minor characters such as storekeepers and townspeople…the barber shop has been used…for the initial confrontation of the hero and the outlaw…the saloon was the place where the forces of good and evil confronted each other…" [175] In the second-season episode, "The Lonely Road," broadcast February 18, 1961, Simon Fry confronts cowboy Trace Phelan first in the barbershop and later in the saloon to tell him to leave a local couple alone or he would be "run clear out of the territory." [176]

In the earliest episodes of *The Deputy*, the general store run by the McCords is a central gathering place. It is where we first see Simon Fry try to trick Clay into helping him, it is where we first bear witness to Clay McCord's reluctance to bear a sidearm, and it is where we first see Fran McCord's concern for her older brother's safety.

Clay and Fran inherited the general store from their widowed mother and it contains a flood of both good and bad memories for them. Their father, Luke, lost his life to violence, and the family's life-blood after his death was the general store. The store contained all food and clothing necessary for the inhabitants of Silver City, right down to the block of cheese Simon Fry often sat down in front of for his supper. Clay worked as a gunsmith in the store, although he refused to work on side arms—only rifles. Not only did Clay oppose side arms himself, but his mother's rule was that there would be no side arms displayed in the store. Clay honored that pledge even after her death. The general store often served as a gathering spot for local townspeople, keeping the McCords heavily involved in the civic affairs of Silver City.

In later episodes, following the events depicted in "The Truly Yours," when outlaws burn down the store and cripple Herk Lamson, the main gathering place for the characters becomes the Silver City marshal's office. Lamson retired and his character is never seen again (with the exception of the episode "Ma Mack," which was broadcast out of sequence at the end of the first season), and Fran McCord moves to Kansas City. Clay chooses to become the full-time deputy marshal in Herk's place because he needs a paying job if he is to rebuild the store.

As seen by the series Writer's Guide, the inhabitants of the Arizona Territory in 1880 are the descendants of the wild-and-wooly settlers who first came west. Gunplay and hard riding have been replaced in many communities by a greater sense of permanence, and an interest in the establishment of law and order. But there remains a struggle between the old ways and the new ways, and it is this struggle the principal characters of *The Deputy* were often pitted against. As stated in the Writer's Guide:

Allen Case and Henry Fonda. (Western TV Photos)

> There is an element, represented by Simon Fry, which bridges the fierce dichotomy between old and new... Pressed to contain the characteristics that would have made him at home among the hard- riding, hard-shoot-ing pioneers and early ranchers, Fry must adopt princi-ples of conduct and method that are foreign to him. [177]

Clay, on the other hand, more clearly represents the new genera-tion, and he, "while anxious to avoid gun-play or violence, must often resort to a quick draw and an accurate sight." [178]

For example, in the episode "Man of Peace," broadcast on De-cember 19, 1959 as episode fourteen of season one, Fry calls on the cavalry for help when he hears Apache Indians have been stealing guns. Clay is outraged that Fry might use military force without first trying to talk things out. He goes on an unarmed peace-keeping mis-sion to talk to the Indians and manages to discover the truth of what happened—the guns were stolen as protection against white men who have been murdering and scalping the Apaches—before blood is spilled. Clay has to fight his way out of trouble with the evil- doers, and has to kill one of them, though he tries to hide this last fact from Fry. As Simon himself notes at the end, "That's Clay McCord. He'll fight harder to keep the peace than most folks would to win a war, and then hide the fact he'd got himself into a fight over it." [179]

But if Simon Fry and Clay McCord represented typical western heroes, so, too, did they encounter typical western antagonists in the stories on *The Deputy*. During the two-season run of the series, Fry and McCord ran into trouble against the same sorts of outlaws, gamblers, con men, *femme fatales*, and tin horns that populated the televi-sion western in the 1950s.

Silver City was depicted as a fast-growing community, a "vola-tile cross-roads for many elements of the old, rough form of life that has yet to be tamed," according to the Writer's Guide. "Simon Fry's position as chief marshal of the territory brings to him, and conse-quently to Clay, many problems and situations that would normally not plague a small town." [180]

In "Backfire," episode sixteen of the first season, an outlaw breaks out of the territorial prison and goes hunting for the man who testi-fied against him in court—Simon Fry. The hunt takes him to Silver City, where Herk Lamson has to kill him by shooting him in the back. Lamson finds that he has lost the respect of the town. When the out-law's grieving widow hires a killer to take revenge on Lamson, Clay must kill the hired gun to protect Lamson.

Of course, once Clay pinned the deputy marshal's badge on per-manently in the later episodes of season one, trouble had a way of finding him even without Fry's help.

BOUNDARIES AND LIMITS

What the Writer's Guide described as "boundaries and limits" had more to do with female characters than anything else.

Neither Simon Fry nor Clay McCord was married, and Herk Lamson was a widower. The Writer's Guide made it clear that there would be "no entangling alliances unless some specific exception is to be made." [181] The lead characters were to be generally attracted by and attractive to women, but nothing permanent—that would, after all, represent a format change.

In "Hang the Law," the 17th episode of the first season, and broadcast January 9, 1960, Simon romances Joy Cartwright (Martha Hyer) as a means to get information that will help him free Clay, who's been imprisoned in a border town on a trumped-up murder charge, but there is no lasting relationship.

Both Clay and Simon were depicted as having plenty of interest in women, however. Both characters romanced Lucy Ballance (Patrice Wymore) in the eighth episode of season two, "Passage to New Orleans" (November 19, 1960), while escorting her to testify at a trial.

STYLE

The stories told in episodes of *The Deputy* were fictional narratives with an eye toward actual history. The producers hoped that writers would keep in mind the way people in the Arizona territory talk, the way they dressed, and their customs and beliefs so that the stories would be authentic. [182]

The producers hoped that the attitudes of the people, their dress and customs, their problems, and all pertinent story points, would be told realistically, as they might have happened in 1880. The language, slang, mannerisms of speech, and action of characters were to be consistent with the southwest part of Arizona. While most stories would take place close to Silver City, other stories would take the principal characters to different locations.

In the first-season episode "The Return of Simon Fry," for example, Clay, Fran, and Herk travel to Prescott, Simon's base of operations, when they believe he has been killed in a horse and buggy accident.

Simon, of course, survived the "accident," which was actually a struggle between Simon and a man trying to kill him. The remainder of the episode is spent in and around Prescott, with the characters trying to solve the mystery of Simon's would-be assassin.

In the second-season episode, "The Jason Harris Story," Simon, Clay, and Sergeant Tasker journey to the nearby town of Hondo, where Simon must arrest the marshal there on charges he tried to help outlaws steal a gold shipment.

In both of these episodes, the scope of the storytelling possibilities is widened by taking the characters to other parts of the territory, outside of Silver City.

PLOT

The Deputy featured all of the motifs and storylines so common among the westerns seen on network television and in syndication during the 1950s and 1960s.

In terms of motifs—those concepts that are seen repeatedly in the literature of a culture—the western on television was full of familiar character types, incidents, and other ideas that were commonly seen, series to series. [183]

Characters commonly seen in the television western were outlaws, marshals/sheriffs, cowboys, *femme fatales*, con artists, greenhorns, cowards, and bad men trying to go straight.

Common incidents inside stories included the gunfight/duel; the train, bank, or stagecoach robbery; a kidnapping; and escape from harm.

Common storylines included ideas such as bigotry, bravery, cowardice, revenge, and frontier justice. Common narratives included tales of the cavalry, the Native-American, homesteaders, cattlemen versus farmers, corruption, and the hero taking a stand for the greater good.

The Deputy used all of these common elements in building its narratives. In the first-season episode, "Like Father," a hired gunman is after the Silver City veterinarian. In "Lawman's Blood," also from the first season, outlaws kidnap Silver City's doctor to treat their gang leader, who was shot by Simon Fry. Both episodes featured characters (frontier outlaws, cowboys), motifs (revenge), and plots (Lamson and McCord standing against outlaws) familiar to fans of western film and television series.

In *The Deputy* we see the con man ("The X Game"), the heroic sheriffs ("Duty Bound"), corruption, as protection racketeers move into Silver City ("Queen Bea"), famous outlaws ("The Big Four" includes Billy the Kid and Ike Clanton), and the bad man trying to set his life right ("The Example," in which an outlaw is afraid his son wants to be like him).

Literary scholars have long pointed out, of course, that in the end there are just a handful of plots, or dramatic situations, that writers have at their disposal, whether they're writing a western series episode or a Broadway play. How many there are, exactly, depends upon the scholar you consult (Western author Frank Gruber believed there were seven plots in Western films). [184] The trick is how a writer will use the common and familiar characteristics, which are part of what's interesting and attractive to viewers about series television, and put them to different uses in terms of character exploration.

The attempted murder of a marshal is not, in other words, a new idea for a story; the key is to take this common storyline and use it to examine the characters in that storyline.

In "The Return of Simon Fry," episode twenty from the first season, Simon is targeted for death. A greedy businessman hires a gunman to kill Simon so that the marshal won't stop a land swindle. Simon escapes the assassination attempt, but feigns his death so that he can discover who wanted him dead and why. Simon's "death" and subsequent investigation are used as opportunities to see how Clay, Fran, and Herk react to the news and what they really thought of Simon. Fran, for example, has made it clear in prior episodes that she views Simon as a bad influence on her brother Clay and that she'd rather Clay not get involved in law enforcement situations with Simon at all.

But by the close of "The Return of Simon Fry," it is clear that much of this attitude is pretense and that in reality she cares deeply for Simon. Not that Fran would admit as much publicly—she goes so far as to say she'd rather not have Simon join the family for dinner. Simon's smile tells the viewer he doesn't believe her protests, either.

THEME

If there was an overriding theme to the television western, it was that good must overcome evil. Time and time again, this theme was played out in episodes of television westerns.

This was no less true in *The Deputy* than it was in any other western series. Simon and Clay opposed outlaws and villains of all kinds as they tried to maintain the peace. In "The Deathly Quiet," the 34th episode of season two and broadcast on May 27, 1961, outlaws have stolen a Gatling gun and it must be recovered. Simon, Clay, and Sarge Tasker put their lives on the line to protect the people of the territory.

But the producers of *The Deputy* also had other aspirations. They also wanted to "illustrate the vast differences in attitudes, aspirations, and behavior between the current generation with those that went before" in the Arizona Territory of 1880, and to focus on "the pioneering spirits pitted against the monumental problem of establishing some degree of permanency and order in a new and growing west." [185]

The idea, unique among television westerns and other drama and literature of the 1950s and early 1960s, was to show youth in a good light, and to demonstrate how new ideas and institutions can be built by starting with "the exuberance of youth and inexperience." [186]

"Show the kid," Fonda said repeatedly to directors.

It was hoped that many stories would focus on the idealism of a youthful society, as personified by Clay McCord and his family, and how that idealism could help build a new structure in which people could live in peace.

In episode twelve of the first season, "The Deal," Clay and Fry must figure out a way to free Fran McCord from an outlaw gang that has kidnapped her to blackmail Clay into helping them rob a local mine. Clay tries to follow the gang leader's orders to get Fry out of town, but Fry guesses the truth, and the two instead team up to break up the gang and rescue Fran. There is a heated debate between Clay and Simon over whether the plan is putting Fran's life in danger, but Simon reminds Clay that the lives of the miners are at stake, as well. In the end, Fran shows herself to be as capable as any of the men by breaking free and clubbing her captor with a frying pan.

The importance of youth and second chances is seen in the first-season episode "The Two Faces of Bob Claxton," in which the McCords take in sixteen-year-old Bob Claxton after he is wounded in a hold-up of the Silver City bank staged by him and his brothers. Fry hopes to lure in the rest of the Claxton brothers gang by holding the boy; Fran McCord hopes to set the boy on the right path.

Recurrent themes were that teamwork and cooperation led to success; that ideals such as honesty, courage, and friendship helped to build community; and that if youth is dedicated to a goal and ideal, it can be as helpful as adults. [187]

SATURDAY NIGHTS ON NBC

As a piece of television programming, *The Deputy* was meant to capitalize on the interest in the western genre then surging on all three major networks. The series was scheduled by NBC to run on Saturday night at 9:00pm.

In 1959, Saturday was the heaviest viewing night of the week for the three networks, [188] and network television as a whole was reaching eight out of every ten persons in the country; eighty million people in all were watching prime-time television.[189]

Half-hour westerns, then dominating the schedule, were being viewed by almost twenty-one percent of all people watching television.[190]

It was into this breach that *The Deputy* walked in the fall of 1959, with a lot of money and viewers at stake. The fall schedule that year was filled with new series in the wake of the quiz scandals; thirty new shows were produced in Hollywood. [191]

Network programming schedules have always been a mix of strategies and contracts; decisions, in the end, are almost always monetary. Some sponsors would agree to sponsor a program, for example, only if it were telecast at 9:00pm; others demanded a certain night of the week. The network programmers themselves had ratings information, and their own gut instincts, telling them where a program would work best.

The research and program departments at NBC didn't want *The Deputy* to be broadcast on Saturday night, describing it was as an "admittedly weak" program [192] (an assessment based in part on the nature of Henry Fonda's involvement). But business concerns countermanded whatever concerns NBC programmers had about the series.

Variety called the series a "reasonably wise media buy." The industry paper said, "Henry Fonda has always been good box office, so a reported $50,000-plus per episode isn't necessarily too much for two bankrollers to split each week." [193] The bankrollers in questions were the sponsors, Kellogg's and General Cigar. Fonda, the paper said, should be able to win a fair cost per thousand.

For the 1959- 60 season, *The Deputy* was up against *Mr. Lucky* on CBS, and the second half of the popular *The Lawrence Welk Show* on ABC. NBC's lead-in program was *Bonanza*, then just starting its 14-year run, followed by *Man and the Challenge*.

The Deputy was one of only four of the thirteen new westerns introduced in the 1959- 60 season to survive into a second year. For the 1960- 61 season, the series was up against the second half of *Checkmate* on CBS and once again the second half of *The Lawrence Welk Show* on ABC. Its lead-ins were *Bonanza*, heading into its second year and rapidly becoming a major hit for the network, and a new program at 8:30pm, *The Tall Man*, another western.

NBC always felt that it could have done better with the series if Henry Fonda had chosen to appear in more episodes. Of course, they would feel this way—and they were probably right. But even without Fonda appearing fully in every episode, NBC still offered the series a third season, which he declined.

CHAPTER FIVE

June and July, 1959

"Trouble ain't long comin', once folks get wind of murder"
— *Marshal Simon Fry*

When the cast and crew of *The Deputy* came together in the middle of 1959 to begin production on what would be the first of two seasons of the series, hopes were high. There was a lot of buzz about the pilot, the series had sold very quickly, and the first set of "Fondas" included good scripts, veteran directors, and exciting guest stars. This period would prove to be one of the creative high-water marks of the series.

As the series went into production, production on the first-season "Fondas" was scheduled first, with the shooting of Fonda's segments in the "Non Fondas" scheduled for later in the summer and into the fall, to wrap up by the middle of October.

Two first-season "Fondas"--"Shadow of the Noose" and "Hang the Law"-- are two of the episodes, along with the pilot, which represented everything the cast and crew hoped the series would be at its best. The episodes focus on a changing west, the rule of law, and the contribution of young people to society. The stories are told with humor and a sense of adventure, but with a minimum of violence.

SHADOW OF THE NOOSE

Depictions of lynching and the mob mentality are staples of the film and television western. The Western, with few exceptions, most notably in "The Virginian," took not only a strong anti-lynching stance, but also frequently spoke against the hysteria that can develop in a mob.

The tension in a western story about a lynching, mob hysteria, or both, comes from the conflict between the forces of good, often represented by a lone individual of the law, and the forces of evil—namely, the mob, even when that mob consists of usually good, well-intentioned people. The mob is seen as a threat to law and order, the establishment of justice on the frontier, and civil society itself. The mob often forms after an act of violence against an innocent, and is whipped into frenzy by one or two townspeople who are blind to the damage they're doing to the very society they claim to represent by taking the law into their own hands.

This tension was the heart of the story told in Roland Kibbee's excellent teleplay, "Shadow of the Noose," directed by Robert B. Sinclair and presented as the fourth episode of the first season of *The Deputy*. Confronted by angry townspeople as he tries to escort a murder suspect out of town, Marshal Fry tells them, "I'm speakin' for the law and the law don't regard trials as a waste of time *or* money."[194]

Henry Fonda was no stranger to the western tale of mob violence. He starred in what is perhaps the definitive motion picture depiction of the impact of lynching on frontier life, *The Ox-Bow Incident*, based on the novel by Walter Van Tilburg Clark and released in 1942 (and a film Fonda spoke highly of). Of course, Fonda was also acquainted with lynching in real life; when he was a boy, his father had taken him to witness one in Omaha in 1919 from the safety of the father's printing plant. Fonda called it the most horrendous thing he'd ever seen.[195]

Henry Fonda as Simon Fry, another unique Fonda characterization. (Western TV Photos)

There are also strong anti-lynching themes in many other productions, including Fonda's own films *The Tin Star* and *Young Mister Lincoln*, in which Lincoln helps protect two suspects. *Two Rode Together*, *The Unforgiven*, and *Johnny Guitar* are among the other films featuring a lynching as part of the narrative. The lynch mob is also prominent in the stories of several television westerns, including *Cimarron Strip* and *The Adventures of Kit Carson*.

SHADOW OF THE NOOSE: THE STORY

The narrative begins with Simon lazily heading back to his headquarters in Prescott after helping to break in a new marshal in Meadsville. Simon is mounted on his horse and riding up a mountain road when suddenly a buckboard races past him, heading downhill the other way. The driver, a young farmer, is slumped over lifelessly, with a bullet in his heart, as the horses race.

Simon chases the buckboard down but sees immediately that the man is dead. He also sees a woman's bonnet and other items on the floor of the buckboard—making him think a woman was pulled from the wagon. Two screams from a woman are heard off in the distance, followed by a gunshot. Simon, who never dismounted, races up the mountain road.

Simon pulls his Winchester and races up over the knoll and scans the area. He rides down the thicket, dismounts, and sees the legs of a woman sticking out from the underbrush. Simon knows right away what this means: "All killings are bad, but this was the worst kind. A lawman's problem wasn't just gettin' the man who did it—it was gettin' him to trial afterward."[196]

Thinking about the people who would be moved to take the law into their own hands, Simon kneels and checks the boot and hoof prints. He sees that the horse's left forefoot has a broken shoe. Simon decides that the killer would head to the nearest town—Oresburg— because he'd need a drink "real bad." [197]

Oresburg is a small, drabby town, with a single saloon. Simon rides into town and ties his mount up outside the saloon. It is nighttime. Checking a nearby horse, Simon sees the broken shoe.

Simon enters the saloon, "unhurried and methodical," [198] and surveys the scene—the usual assortment of barflies, cowhands, and local characters, drab, like their town, with one exception—the Drifter Simon sees drinking alone at the bar. The Drifter has clearly been on the road for days; he is dirty and dusty.

Simon puts the Drifter under arrest and expertly takes his gun; his hope is to get the man out of the saloon without raising a stir. Unfortunately, the Drifter begins to loudly defend himself and make claims that he is innocent of the shooting. He was in the hills, yes, but he didn't do it—he ran because he knew he'd be a suspect.

The townspeople begin to gather as Simon escorts the Drifter out of the saloon and directs him toward the jail. The crowd follows, demanding that the Drifter be allowed to talk. They are angry, as Simon knew they would be, over the murders, especially the murder of the woman.

Simon locks the man up in jail and waits through the night. He decides that Oresburg isn't safe for the trial and decides to take the Drifter to Prescott. As they mount, the townspeople, with Akins as their leader and chief spokesman, gather around the horses at the hitching rail. Akins says, "We don't hold with woman- killin' in these parts, Marshal."

"Don't know of any parts where folks do," Simon answers. [199]

Simon tells the crowd that he will consider any attempt to take the prisoner a criminal offense and that he will shoot to kill. The townspeople know he means it.

Simon escorts the Drifter out of town, with the townspeople following at a distance. The Drifter complains that Simon is a stickler for the law. "Where would you be right now if I wasn't?" Simon asks him. [200]

Simon, tired and sleepy on the trail, decides to divert to Silver City where he hopes to get Clay's help in getting the prisoner to Prescott. The crowd follows the two men into Silver City, where Clay and Fran protest that Simon has not only brought the Drifter into town, but into their store.

Clay is unconvinced that his help is needed, and tells Simon that he won't go along. It isn't until his sister Fran speaks to him about it that Clay changes his mind. Fran, who believes the Drifter may be innocent, wonders if the man can even get a fair trial and wants to make certain he can get safely to Prescott.

Simon locks the prisoner up in the Silver City jail overnight so that he can sleep, but Akins, still the leader of the mob, slips the Drifter a gun through the jail window, and the Drifter breaks past Herk Lamson and out of jail. Only the intervention of Clay, warned about the escape by his young brother Brandy, prevents the Drifter from being caught by the mob. Simon places Akins under arrest, and he and Clay get ready to transport the Drifter out of town.

The trio is followed by what remains of the mob, minus its leader, and Simon and Clay have to fight it off one last time, out on the trail. It is then that Simon tells Clay that he knows the Drifter is guilty because he saw the man pump bullets into the murdered woman as he rode to the top of the knoll to investigate.

"You let my sister think he was innocent!" Clay yells at him.

"That's her privilege until after the trial," Simon answers.

"And, of course, she might've felt differently about me ridin' along if she knew he was guilty." [201]

The mob defeated, and justice ready to be served once they arrived in Prescott, Simon climbs into his bedroll for some sleep.

SHADOW OF THE NOOSE: THE PRODUCTION

The script for "Shadow of the Noose" called for the regular first-season cast at full muster—Simon, Clay, Fran, Herk, and Brandy were all seen in the story. In addition, several guest stars were needed for the story, most prominently the roles of Akins, the big landowner near Oresburg, and the Drifter, the young man arrested by Marshal Fry on suspicion of murder. *The Deputy* was fortunate in its selection of the first-rate actors cast, as they added depth to the story.

Denver Pyle was already an old hand at the Western by the time he played Akins, the owner of "a big spread" who riles up the townspeople, creating the lynch fever. He had been working in Hollywood for twelve years, and had played character parts in dozens of films and television shows, including bit parts in films like *Drum Beat* with Alan Ladd and *Johnny Guitar* with Joan Crawford, and television programs such as *Annie Oakley* and *Fury,* among many, many others. Four years earlier, in 1955, Pyle was not only a finalist for the role of Marshal Matt Dillon on the television version of *Gunsmoke,* but he had been told he had the job. Then James Arness tested, had the part, and played it for twenty years. Pyle was consistent and reliable in his performances throughout his long career in Hollywood, which ended with his death in 1997. As director Burt Kennedy said of him,

"People know him as Uncle Jesse on *The Dukes of Hazzard,* but he's done other things that were very good." [202]

Actor Clu Gulager was eight years younger than Denver Pyle, and somehow looked even younger than his thirty years, when he was cast as "The Drifter." He had been working in Hollywood for three years when he performed in "Shadow of the Noose," the first of his two appearances on *The Deputy.* Like Pyle, Gulager had been making the rounds of 1950s television guest appearances in everything from *Studio One* and *Westinghouse Desilu Playhouse* to *Laramie* and *Wanted: Dead or Alive.* In the 1960s he had co-starring roles on a pair of westerns, *The Tall Man* and *The Virginian,* and left his mark on many series in the following years.

The other secondary character roles on the episode—members of the mob, various townspeople, the bartender—were filled with other actors who often appeared in these kinds of roles in television programs, including William Henry as the 1ˢᵗ Outrider and John McKee as Marshal Hollister.

They all signed aboard and went to work for the director of the episode, Robert B. Sinclair.

By the time he was chosen to direct "Shadow of the Noose," Bob Sinclair had been directing in Hollywood for more than twenty years, and he brought a wealth of film and stage experience with him to *The Deputy* that summer of 1959.

Sinclair was born in Toledo, Ohio, on May 24, 1905, and graduated from the Wharton School of Business Administration at the University of Pennsylvania in 1926.

He began on Broadway in 1930, as stage manager for the play *Once in a Lifetime,* and went on to direct some of the most successful

Broadway productions of the 1930s, including *Life Begins, Dodsworth, Pride and Prejudice, The Postman Always Rings Twice, The Women, Babes in Arms,* and *The Philadelphia Story.* In all, he directed or staged nineteen Broadway productions between 1930 and 1951. He moved from New York City to Beverly Hills in 1938, and signed with MGM as a director; in the sum of his career he achieved less acclaim in Hollywood than he had in the theater, but he worked consistently in film and television through the early 1960s.

His first two films were *Woman Against Woman* and *Dramatic School* in 1938, and he subsequently directed a series of mostly modest productions, including *Down in San Diego* (1941), *Mr. and Mrs. North* (1942), and *Mr. District Attorney* (1947), before moving on to become a prolific director of series television in the 1950s. He worked in a wide variety of genres in episodic television, including westerns, detective programs, police dramas, and anthologies.

Bob Sinclair was in semi-retirement, although active in local theater, when he was murdered in his home in Montecito, CA, on January 3, 1970, during a burglary attempt staged by a college student. His wife since 1944, actress Heather Angel, witnessed the attack but was uninjured herself. The stage, film, and television director was only 64 at the time of his murder.

For *The Deputy,* Sinclair directed seven full episodes himself, as well as the Fonda segments in several other episodes. "Shadow of the Noose" was his first, and Sinclair's contribution to the episode was critical. He tells the story well, and his visuals help bring the characters and story to life.

Production on "Shadow of the Noose" was scheduled for three days, June 17- 19, 1959, following two days of scheduled rehearsal, on

June 15 and June 16. [203] The scheduled rehearsal days in television at that time often involved mostly wardrobe fittings and such; shooting this half-hour episode in three days was also standard for the time. Locations would include Laramie Street, the Laramie Ranch, and the Western Street at Universal. Interiors would include the sets already established as the McCord General Store and the Silver City Marshal's Office, along with two other sets for this episode, the saloon in Oresburg and the Oresburg Marshal's Office. [204]

Episodes of television series, like motion pictures, are not shot in sequence. They are shot in the most efficient way possible to save time and money. Generally speaking, that means, for example, that when the production team sets up at an interior set or an exterior location, all the scenes in that location will be shot while the cast and crew are there. The episode is then assembled in the proper order during the editing process.

The challenge for the actor in episodic television, then, is to find the character in a series of takes, on a set, while working long hours, and while shooting scenes out of sequence, even though those scenes may often connect in the narrative. It is an inherently different experience than working in the theater, where the play is run straight through, and there is an audience that is feeding the energy of the performance.

In the case of "Shadow of the Noose," the script covered 106 scenes in about thirty-four pages of script. Bob Sinclair's job was to bring the script in on time, and on budget, with as much creativity and dramatic punch as possible.

The first day of shooting was Wednesday, June 17. Shooting was scheduled to begin at 8:00am and the goal was to shoot nearly thirteen pages of the script that day, all on interiors, including the McCord General Store, the Silver City Marshal's Office, the Oresburg Saloon, and the Oresburg Marshal's Office. [205]

The first set-up was the interior for the McCord General Store for scenes 56- 67, the part of the story where Simon and the drifter ask Clay to help Herk and Brandy also enters to talk to Simon.

Needed on the set for these shots were Henry Fonda, Clu Gulager, Allen Case, Betty Lou Keim, Wally Ford, and Gary Hunley. Also present was a welfare worker for young Mr. Hunley.

The props department had to make certain that everything needed in these scenes was present and ready, including the hat with the bullet hole, Herk's shotgun, apples, a rifle, dresses, a dress box, and the box marked "Poison" where Clay stored his sidearm and deputy's badge.

And so on it went throughout that first day of shooting. Work was completed on the following scenes, filmed in this order:

> Brandy wakes up Herk in the Silver City Marshal's Office;
>
> The drifter reacts offstage to Akins while Simon Sleeps;
>
> The drifter knocks Herk out and runs;
>
> Brandy sees Akins pass his gun to the drifter;
>
> Simon arrests the drifter in the Oresburg Saloon;
>
> Simon brings the drifter into the Oresburg Marshal's Office and calls to Hollister;
>
> Still inside the Oresburg Marshal's Office, Simon tells the drifter they are threatened with lynching.

A total of just under thirteen pages was shot that first day—needless to say, a much faster pace than in the motion pictures Fonda had worked on. [206]

The goal for the second day, June 18, was to shoot just under twelve pages of the script—another full day of work for all involved. On this day, the crew moved to exterior locations, including the Western Street representing Silver City (exteriors of the general store, Herk Lamson's office, the livery stable, the street, and the saloon), and Laramie Street, representing the Oresburg Saloon and Marshal's Office. [207]

The second day of production included the following scenes on the Western Street, shot in this sequence:

Establishing shots of Silver City;

Akins tells the mob to keep watch, and rides out, as Brandy exits the general store;

Akins and the mob are joined by Silver City townspeople in front of the general store;

Clay exits the general store, followed by Brandy and Fran;

Brandy enters the Marshal's Office;

Brandy brings up the horses from the livery stable to Simon and the Drifter;

Akins and the mob exit the Silver City Saloon and approach the marshal's office;

Outside the Silver City Marshal's Office, Brandy sees Akins empty his gun and head to the back of the jail. Brandy follows him;

Brandy runs back to the McCord General Store;

Akins rejoins the mob;

Outside the Marshal's Office, the Drifter starts for his horse, but is stopped by Akins and the mob;

Clay halts the proceedings by shooting the heel of the Drifter's boot;

Brandy runs to get Simon and Herk.

The crew then moved to the Laramie Street location, sitting in for Oresburg, and shot the scenes outside of the Oresburg Saloon and Marshal's Office, in this order:

Simon riding in, checking over the horse, and entering the saloon;

Akins asking Simon to let the Drifter talk;

The Drifter talking;

Simon and the Drifter entering the marshal's office;

Simon and the Drifter being threatened by the mob as they depart.

Work on day two included the filming of about eleven and 5/8 pages of script. [208]

Day three, June 19, was relatively calm by the standards set the previous two days—"just" nine and 3/8 pages of script. The crew shot all the scenes at the Laramie Ranch and a nearby roadway, in this order:

Simon and the Drifter at their campfire watching the mob at its campfire;

The mob following Simon and the Drifter in open country;

Simon and the Drifter ride over the crest of the hill;

At the trail camp, Simon tells Clay the Drifter is guilty;

A member of the mob sees Simon and the Drifter offstage and yells;

The mob gets drunk and noisy, then mounts and rides;

Simon finds the dead woman;

Simon stops the runaway wagon.

The last sequence shot was actually the first scenes in the story, scenes 1-9, as Simon chases and then stops the runaway wagon in the opening teaser and notes that "the loafin' was over." [209]

The loafing was hardly over, either, for the editors and other members of the production team which then took all of the film shot between June 17 and 19 and assembled it in time for its showing on NBC. "Shadow of the Noose" was broadcast as the fourth episode of season one, on October 3, 1959.

SHADOW OF THE NOOSE: IN PERSPECTIVE

Bob Sinclair's direction keeps the story moving briskly and brings out the points Roland Kibbee wanted to make with his script—the long shot of the mob trailing Simon and the Drifter as they leave Oresburg; Clay wearing his store apron as he shoots the Drifter's heel off; and Fry's heroic stature, methodically tracking and arresting the suspect.

Roland Kibbee's script has the hallmarks which he hoped would make *The Deputy* unique among the television westerns of the time—

a focus on family and youth; an examination of the importance of law and order in a changing west, as the old ways gave way to the new; a sense of humor; and the presence of Henry Fonda.

"Shadow of the Noose" emphasizes family, youth, and community through the interaction of Simon with the McCord family in Silver City. As he tries to convince Clay to join him, Simon knows that deep down Clay is struggling with his conscience—he feels a deep commitment to help, but is held back by his responsibilities to his family and the promises he has made to stay out of harm's way. Clay's abhorrence of violence, and his disgust with the lynch mob fever, is what help him decide that to help protect his family and community in this case, he is needed at Simon Fry's side.

Fran and Brandy side with Simon, too, although for different reasons. Brandy clearly looks up to the marshal and is eager to help once he realizes that the Drifter has had help in making a jailbreak, the well-intentioned child representing hope for the future. Fran, on the other hand, wants to see justice served and, in a change of her usual heart on the matter, urges Clay to help. Clay's expertise with firearms—he shoots the heel off the Drifter's boot to prevent him from escaping in Silver City— helps establish him as both a force to be reckoned with and a force for good in the community. All of these young people, through their actions, are helping Silver City grow and are contributing to the building of a safer community in the West.

The themes of good versus evil, and the stresses put on Silver City and other towns by the changing conditions in the West, are clearly evident. Murder cannot be tolerated and must be punished, but punished not through more violence as in the old days but through the law, represented by Simon Fry. Marshal Fry is known throughout the territory as a dedicated lawman and is so respected that he is referred to as "Mr. Fry." His actions and words make this clear; he not only brings the suspect to justice, but knows he must do so while preventing the lynch mob from taking over. "There were people who waited for crimes like this," he says, "so's they'd have an excuse to satisfy their own lust for violence." [210]

HANG THE LAW

One of the major creative challenges facing the producers of any television series is how to maintain the series' "voice" in scripts written by writers other than the series creators. The characters, tone, and premise have to remain consistent. Herb Purdom's first story for the series was an almost perfect match to the series pilot in terms of its tone, and it stands as one of the best episodes of the series.

Purdom accumulated writing credits in several different genres during his career as a television writer, including westerns (*Broken Arrow*), medical shows (*Emergency!*), and private detective shows (*Hawaiian Eye*). Also a novelist, he won a Spur Award in 1966 from the Western Writers of America for his work *Brother John*. He wrote seven episodes of *The Deputy*.

HANG THE LAW: THE STORY

In "Hang the Law," Clay is arrested on trumped-up murder charges in the border town of Ludlow, a community outside Simon's jurisdiction. When Fry arrives to help, he runs smack into trouble with Blanche Niles, the elderly town matriarch and a local ranch owner, who describes Fry as "Filthy as a prairie dog, unshaven, cool, nervy. A gunfighter if I ever saw one." [211]

Later, she pulls out a pepperbox pistol, disarms Fry, and orders him to drop his gun belt. Simon tells Clay, "Well, she ain't exactly a lady. Fact is as a gunslinger she's pure lightning and seventeen claps of thunder." Clay is astounded that she took Simon's gun away. "Well, you want the truth," Simon says, "A woman and a gun about scares me to death." [212]

Simon verbally jousts with both the local constable and the Ludlow Citizen's Committee, including Blanche Niles, hoping to get Clay released before he hangs. Simon traces the witnesses against Clay to the Ludlow Revival Hall, where he meets Joy Cartwright, the sister of the Reverend Cartwright.

Simon is immediately suspicious of the Reverend and his so-called converts, most of whom look like gunslingers. By romancing Joy, Simon learns that the Revival Hall is really a cover for a cattle rustling operation being run by Reverend Cartwright and others against local ranchers, including Blanche Niles. The mistake the gang makes is in framing Clay for murder, believing he was in town on business as a deputy to Simon Fry; however, Clay had been in town only to see about setting up a second general store. The framing of Clay McCord leads to the undoing of the Reverend Cartwright and his cattle rustlers. Simon and Clay, with a big assist from Blanche Niles, outgun the rustlers in a gunfight at the end of the episode. All of the rustlers, as well as Joy Cartwright, are arrested and jailed, and Clay is proven innocent.

In addition to the wonderful scenes between the characters of Simon Fry and Blanche Niles (sometimes referred to as Blanche Miles), the episode also features strong scenes between Simon and Clay in

Clay's jail cell, and between Simon and Joy Cartwright as the chief marshal, relieved of his gun, resorts to cunning and trickery through the "tête-à-tête, a well-planned seduction" [213] of Joy.

The episode is great fun, as Simon demonstrates the depth of his friendship with Clay by galloping across Arizona to help his young friend. Herb Purdom's script displays a sense of humor true to the "non-western Western" formula created by Roland Kibbee and Norman Lear, while giving every major character his or her scene, and throws in an action sequence at the end of the episode to boot. The gunplay at the end of the episode is, however, more of a concession to the network television appetite for action than anything else, at least in terms of its connection to the story. Even so, during the gun battle, Simon and Clay bicker back and forth, with Simon complaining about a bullet crease in his new gun belt.

The only series regulars in "Hang the Law" are Simon and Clay; all others are guest performers. Like "Shadow of the Noose," this episode featured excellent performances from the guest stars, including Martha Hyer (Joy), who also sings in the episode; Lillian Bronson (Blanche); Willard Sage (Reverend Cartwright); Grant Richards (Frank Ivy); and Robert Armstrong (Constable Dobbs).

Hyer and Bronson, especially, are stand-outs in the episode. Hyer was a rising star in Hollywood, mixing in television appearances between film assignments; she had co-starred in *Some Came Running* in 1958, in which Betty Lou Keim also appeared, and was Oscar-nominated for her part. Bronson was a long-time character actor in Hollywood; by the time she was cast in *The Deputy*, Bronson had accumulated credits in films and television for more than fifteen years.

Not all casting decisions run precisely true to what is written in a script. In Herb Purdom's script for "Hang the Law," Constable Dobbs, the peace officer appointed by the Ludlow Citizens Committee, is described as a "sturdy frontiersman with fierce mustaches and a buckskin coat." [214] As played by Robert Armstrong, Dobbs comes across as anything but a sturdy frontiersman; the emphasis given the character is instead found is the play given to his obvious subservience to Blanche Niles.

HANG THE LAW: THE PRODUCTION

"Hang the Law," originally titled "Framed," went into production about a month after shooting had been completed on "Shadow of the Noose," and was also directed by Bob Sinclair, one of the major creative forces in the earliest days of the series. The rehearsal day on "Hang the Law" was July 21, 1959, a Tuesday, with shooting scheduled over the following three days—Wednesday, July 22; Thursday, July 23, and Friday, July 24.

The demands of the story included twelve characters; three exterior sets (Ludlow Street, where Clay is arrested; several locations in the range around Ludlow; and Split Rock Canyon, where Simon and Clay break up an ambush planned by the cattle rustlers); and four interior sets (the Ludlow Jail, where Clay is under lock and key; the Revival Hall, where Simon first meets Joy; the private hotel room, where Simon romances Joy; and the banker's office, where Simon confronts the Ludlow Citizens Committee).

On the first day of production, Sinclair would put his cast and crew through the paces of almost twelve pages of script, shooting on Laramie Street (standing in as Ludlow's main street), at the Revival Hall, banker's office, and jail sets, and out on the range locations.

Day two was an even busier day, with more than fourteen pages of script shot, all of it in the set doubling as the Ludlow Jail.

Friday, the third day of production, was the "slow" day, with just under ten pages of script shot at Split Rock Canyon, in the range locations, and in the private hotel room. In all, Herb Purdom's script totaled thirty-one and 1/8 pages of story.

The production schedule for "Hang the Law" was largely dictated by one important story point—Simon's shaving of the three-day growth of beard on his face when he makes the decision to seduce Joy Cartwright to discover the truth of both Clay's arrest and the rustling activities in Ludlow. This meant that all of the scenes with Simon's bearded face had to be done first, and all the shots featuring a clean-shaven Simon had to be shot after that. It is a point Bob Sinclair clearly makes in his shooting schedule for the show—it comes about midway through the second day of shooting. [215]

The speed of filming and pace of production in this episode were very similar to "Shadow of the Noose" and the other "Fondas" produced during the late spring and summer of 1959 (and, for that matter, again in the summer of 1960 during the production of season two). But whereas "Shadow of the Noose" aired early in the first season, "Hang the Law" would not air until midseason, the following January, as per a decision by NBC to sprinkle the six "Fondas" through the first-season schedule.

POSTSCRIPT

In these two early "Fondas," produced in June and July 1959, Henry Fonda is every inch the western hero he was in films such as *The Tin*

A not unworthy addition to the Fonda canon. (Western TV Photos)

Star. His Simon Fry is deliberate, expert, and moves gracefully, coiled as if ready to spring into needed action at any moment (as he did in his meeting with the Ludlow Citizens Committee, grabbing a local citizen when the banker insinuated that Simon would allow Clay to escape from custody). Simon Fry is dignified, honest, and incorruptible, even when threatened by a mob or fatigue.

The character in *The Deputy* is set apart from earlier Fonda western portrayals, however, by the sense of humor and irony resting next door to his sense of duty— namely, his gentle con of the McCords in "Shadow of the Noose" and his unapologetic con of Joy Cartwright in "Hang the Law" to help free Clay. As seen in "Shadow of the Noose" and "Hang the Law," two outstanding first-season episodes of *The Deputy,* Simon Fry stands tall among film and television western characters and is a not unworthy addition to the Fonda canon.

CHAPTER SIX

That was the Arizona Territory

To fully understand *The Deputy*, it is helpful to look at Henry Fonda's experience with his second primetime series, *The Smith Family*, which aired on ABC- TV from January 1971 until June 1972.

Fonda played a police detective, Chad Smith, and the series focused mostly on his home life and how his job impacted that domestic setting. Smith was happily married, with three children. Fonda said that part of the appeal for him was that the series reminded him of "The Commissioner," the book upon which his 1968 crime film, *Madigan*, had been based, although the film switched perspectives from the commissioner to the police detective, played by Richard Widmark. The book had focused a great deal on the home life of the police commissioner, and how his job intruded upon and affected life at home.

"We do have shows where I'm doing a cop's work," Fonda said at the time. "But it is all in relation to the family. My wife is played by Janet Blair, and we are the parents of three kids ranging in age from 7 to 18.

"It's essentially a family story, what it's like to be the family of a cop." [216]

Fonda also landed the same type of production schedule that had attracted him to *The Deputy* in 1959, except that the system that had been tried by the producers of the western in 1959 had since been perfected by producer Don Fedderson in situation comedies starring Brian Keith and Fred MacMurray. Under the deal, Fonda would work about fifteen weeks on the show, and be free the rest of the year to pursue other projects. In his absence, the rest of the cast, including Darleen Carr, Ron Howard, and Michael James Wixted (as the Smith family children), would shoot all of the scenes not involving the Chad Smith character. The system ran even more smoothly on *The Smith Family* than it had on *The Deputy*, even though Fonda starred fully in every episode of this series, unlike his first.

Fonda was enthusiastic about the series as it premiered. "I believed in the characters and the concept of the show," he said. [217]

Importantly, he had seen fifteen scripts in advance— the opposite experience from *The Deputy*. He had sent a few *Smith Family* scripts back, and asked for changes in a few others, but essentially Fonda was pleased with the scripts and the stories. "It was very much like shooting a film," he said. "And that's not as bad as it sounds." [218]

In fact, the production schedule had worked so well during the first season of the series that fifteen episodes were turned out in just nine weeks. Fonda called it "one of the most pleasant experiences I've ever had in show business." [219]

There was just one problem.

"It was a terrible TV show," Ron Howard said. "It never found its way. It went on for a year and a half because that's the deal they'd made with Henry Fonda." [220]

In recalling working on the series, Howard said he learned a lot about filmmaking from the director Herschel Daugherty, and enjoyed working with Fonda, who was very talkative with the young actor, telling stories about acting and working with directors like John Ford. But, still, Howard said, "The most memorable thing was this theme song we had called 'Primrose Lane.'" [221]

The Smith Family, for all of its superior production planning and its high-caliber cast, was a failure for ABC on Wednesday nights. It was seen as trite, almost painful to watch, in its depiction of the Smiths and their trials and tribulations. It was part of a trend in television programming at the time toward "relevancy" by using then-current social issues as plot points, such as Chad Smith discovering his own daughter at a party where marijuana is being used.

It simply didn't work.

Producer Stephens, who worked often with Don Fedderson, called the series "one of our disaster shows." [222] Creator Edmund Hartmann said, "Who wants to look at the family life of a police officer?" [223]

Fonda had not recalled *The Deputy* fondly to reporters while publicizing his return to network television in 1971. He was quite open about the problems he felt were inherent in his television western, as he had always been about his work projects, while at the same time praising his new show. A year and a half later, however, when the brief run of *The Smith Family* was over, it had produced far fewer episodes (39) than had *The Deputy* (76), and there's no comparison in terms of the quality or the watch-ability of the two series. *The Smith Family* made *The Deputy* look like *My Darling Clementine* by comparison.

Who or what was at fault? The writers? The producers? The network time slot? Fonda?

To paraphrase the standard Hollywood axiom, no one sets out to make a bad television series. It is enormously difficult to pull all of the pieces together and create a successful show. The failures far outnumber the successes.

It has been long known that television has a voracious appetite for program material. As soon as one show is off the air, another must appear. Were shows to grow on trees it would be easier to fill program schedules with high-quality hits. The hope is that lightning will be caught in a bottle, and the right mix of cast, writers, producers, directors, and format will come together to produce a highly-rated, profits-generating, artistic success.

In the end, the miracle of network television of any era, and certainly of the era in which *The Deputy* aired, is that those actors, writers, and producers found a way to produce as many enjoyable television episodes in as many series as they did.

Television playwright Rod Serling, commenting in 1966 on the "total lack of consistency in quality in television series," said, "No writer can be consistently good, week in and week out. It's like asking Arthur Miller to do *Death of a Salesman* every seven days." [224]

The biggest problem facing *The Deputy* was not the basic format, or the production standards, or the casting. The problem, as with a lot of television then and now, was the number of episodes that must be produced in a short time frame. Producing 39 episodes a year, and having to fill the primetime schedule, week after week, made it enormously difficult to come up with enough material to make it all work.

It was a problem that Fonda himself would come to recognize, somewhat belatedly, about weekly television series work in *The Deputy*:

**Allen Case and Henry Fonda, behind the scenes
on Laramie Street. (Milton T. Moore Photos)**

As I should have realized, if I'd stopped to think about it, when you do a half- hour segment in two and a half days—you start one on Monday and finish it on Wednesday noon, and Wednesday afternoon you start your second one—that means two scripts coming through every week. There aren't that many good writers and good scripts. And there's not a backlog of scripts, so that when a script comes, if you don't do that one you close down the production, and you can't afford to close down production. There's no other script to do, so you do the one that's available and try to make it as good as you can—which is a compromise. [225]

In 1959, television was decades away from deciding, as an industry, that fewer episodes were needed to fill out a season. The number would drop over the years to 26, 24, and 22, and even lower in some cases, mostly because of increasing production costs, but it wasn't until *The Sopranos* premiered in 1999 that network television programmers, especially those programming cable networks, began to realize that a reduced number of episodes would mean the creative talent could concentrate more on quality, instead of quantity.

In 1959, the situation Revue faced was that 39 episodes were needed that first season, Fonda would star in only six, and the episodes would need to be produced very quickly. That was the system, and they had to make do. There was never any consideration given, for example, to producing just ten "Fondas," as would have been the case five decades in the future. Nor was anyone suggesting that Revue should produce just six "Fondas" and run those on NBC over the summer schedule—no, here was Henry Fonda in a weekly western series and the weekly schedule was where the money was and that was that. The producers had to find a way to produce 39 and make as many of them work as they could.

Philip Purser, writing in The British Film Institute's *Sight and Sound* that year, put it rather harshly:

> Shortcomings of television film hardly need elaborating. Compared with the feature film it is a conveyer belt product, cheap and hurried. A thirty-minute episode can be turned out in two-and-a-half-days, and Henry Fonda is the only man who has ever deluded himself into believing that the result is even up to a C- picture. (He should take a closer look at some of the cutting between exteriors and studio shots in his own sad investment, *The Deputy*.) [226]

True enough—in shooting a television series in 1959 producers were never going to be able to make it look as unhurried as if the production unit had had a month to shoot in Monument Valley. But on the other hand, *The Deputy* looked better than many of the western series on television during this time; for one thing, it used far fewer painted backdrops than Warner Brothers' westerns such as *Cheyenne* and *Bronco*

Still, Fonda had gone into *The Deputy* with high hopes. [227] He had genuinely liked the pilot script and the character of Simon Fry. He had grown frustrated, his professionalism and experience—not to mention his publicly-stated desire for the money - running head-first into the hurried schedule, with scripts that needed work and corners having to be cut here and there to meet the schedule—a shooting

**Simon Fry (Henry Fonda) at the card table in
"Focus of Doom," a first season "Fonda."**

schedule that was four and five times faster on a television set than it was in film. [228] In theatre—and remember Fonda's first love was the stage— there was one script you could focus on and improve upon. In film, there was one script that you could focus on to improve. In television, one script was good enough for only one episode and another was needed for the next one.

What *The Deputy* needed was more stories from co-creator Roland Kibbee and Norman Lear, who knew those characters so well, not to mention more stories like those written by Herb Purdom, who would go on to win a Spur Award from the Western Writers of America in 1966. While there were good scripts from Richard N. Morgan, who created the Sergeant Tasker character, and writers like Clarke Reynolds, Curtis Kenyon (then head of the Writer's Guild, West), Kay Lenard, Jess Carneol, and line producer Michel Kraike, it is fair to say that, more, higher-quality stories were needed— Fonda was on the money about that.

For example, an episode like "The Choice," about an ex-convict trying to live down his past and become a doctor, made for interesting and entertaining television in 1960, while an episode like "Trail of Darkness," though full of heroic scenes involving Allen Case as Clay McCord, is hard to take seriously because the chief crime boss is seen with a bag over his head to hide his identity.

For additional story material, perhaps the producers could have adapted short stories from established authors such as Ernest Haycox, Louis L'Amour, and Alan Le May, as other western series did. Haycox's work, for example, was used on series such as *Tales from Wells Fargo* and *Cimarron City*.

Watching Henry Fonda, Allen Case, Wally Ford, Betty Lou Keim, and Read Morgan in *The Deputy*, one yearns for better stories on a more consistent basis, seeing what they did with the better material they got.

"I always thought an episodic television writer must be one of the most stressed guys in the world," Read Morgan said. "Because on any given day (the producers) will tell you we've got to have thirteen pages by tonight." [229]

Each series presents its own set of challenges. In the case of *The Deputy*, the other enormous challenge facing the producers and writers was the fact that Fonda wouldn't commit to star in every episode, even as his very presence in the series set the bar so high in the mind of the public that it was hard, under the production terms of the day, to make it work, week after week.

Broadcasting magazine put its finger on the issues facing *The Deputy* in its 1959 fall preview issue:

> Henry Fonda makes an auspicious start with his television debut in *The Deputy*. It's the best new western of the season and should run close to *Have Gun, Will Travel* and *Gunsmoke* among the better cowboy shows.
>
> There's only one reservation. Mr. Fonda is not the deputy. He's the chief marshal of the territory and apparently will bob in and out of the various episodes. While he's there he brings new class to the area of westerns, but when he's out of camera things seem to deteriorate somewhat. [230]

The magazine made it clear the difficulty ahead was not found in Allen Case, who was described as "a sort of Pat Boone of the cowboy set and his clean-cut innocence is an effective foil to Mr. Fonda's unshaven characterization." [231] The problem was the expectations the audience would have because of Henry Fonda's involvement: As the trade magazine noted, "Mr. Fonda gets star billing and deserves it, but he may have to stick around more than he apparently has in mind." [232]

Fonda could have chosen differently, but he didn't. The creative personnel on the series, NBC, and the audience made due with what they got. If Henry Fonda had made the same choice as Barbara Stanwyck did a year later, when she chose to host an anthology series and starred in 32 of the 36 episodes, things would have been even better than they were for *The Deputy*. If Barbara Stanwyck could stand in front of painted backdrops and pretend it was Hong Kong, [233] then it was fine for Henry Fonda to chase outlaws at the Laramie Ranch. She simply chose a different level of involvement than he had.

Then again, the history of major film actors starring on network television in a weekly series is spotty at best. Stanwyck herself failed with her anthology series, though she won an Emmy for her work on it, while her later series, *The Big Valley*, was far more successful in syndication than it was during its run on ABC- TV. Other film stars had trouble with television series. James Stewart (*The Jimmy Stewart Show, Hawkins*), Glenn Ford (*Cade's County, The Family Holvak*), Anthony Quinn (*The Man and the City*), Charlton Heston (*The Colbys*), and Shirley MacLaine (*Shirley's World*) are just a few of the film stars who came a cropper on television (though Robert Taylor did well with *The Detectives Starring Robert Taylor*). There was no guarantee, in other words, that *The Deputy* would have been a major hit in the ratings had Fonda starred in every episode. It didn't, after all, happen with *The Smith Family*.

But in the case of *The Deputy,* the nagging thought is that it would have worked well, that the series could have been a hit, because there is very good and interesting television in those episodes in which Fonda did star all the way through, shared scenes with Allen Case as Clay, and played a major role in the story. Those episodes are fun to watch. It wets the viewer's appetite for what might have been because they were high-quality television western episodes.

Henry Fonda never gave less than his best on the series—any suggestion to the contrary is off the mark. The stories told by Read Morgan, Tay Garnett, and others from the set are testament to that. Fonda, one of the best actors of the 20th century, is a pleasure to watch in *The Deputy,* even if some of the material is less than what one would hope for.

In the end, the major problem with *The Deputy* is that Fonda's name is on the marquee, but he's not around as much as everyone would have liked.

It would still have been great fun for audiences, then and now, had Fonda and the producers reached into a few more Fonda connections for guest stars, such as son Peter Fonda or daughter Jane Fonda, both of whom were just getting started on their careers then. Jane even visited the set in the early days of the series. (Asked in 1960 if his daughter would guest on an episode, Fonda said, "No, she is a star.") [234] Other possibilities included Cathy Downs, Fonda's co-star from *My Darling Clementine,* and even James Stewart, who made occasional guest appearances on television. Fonda and Stewart were paired together all too infrequently in their careers, and here was another opportunity missed.

Given their estrangement at the time, there was never a chance that Fonda and director John Ford could have teamed up again for an

Jane and Henry Fonda, on the set of The Deputy, 1959.
(Allan Grant/Time- Life Pictures/Getty Images)

episode or two. Ford had directed Fonda in those memorable films, including *Grapes of Wrath, Drums Along the Mohawk, Young Mr. Lincoln, Fort Apache,* and *The Fugitive,* but the two proud and stubborn men had argued (Ford had knocked Fonda down, and Fonda called him a "drunken old son of a bitch") on the set of *Mister Roberts,* and the rift wasn't healed for years. [235] Instead, Ford's TV western contribution was limited to "The Colter Craven Story" on *Wagon Train.*

The Deputy was, despite its problems, a cut above many television

Henry Fonda and Allen Case. (Western TV Photos)

westerns of the period, even if the series only occasionally reached the storytelling heights of the very best television westerns, such as *Gunsmoke*, which had the advantage of involvement from co-creator John Meston and his outstanding scripts. *The Deputy* was certainly more languid than high-water marks like *Have Gun, Will Travel, Lawman*, and *The Rifleman*, but on the other hand it had more humor.

The series had reliable direction from old pros such as Tay Garnett, Bob Sinclair, and David Butler.

The series can boast of the list of what director Tay Garnett described as "great guest stars," [236] and the lead performances in the series are fine. All the players—Fonda, Case, Read Morgan, Betty Lou Keim, and Wally Ford-- give solid work.

There is much to enjoy and admire in those 76 old black-and-white episodes of *The Deputy*. Maybe that's enough, in the end.

Henry Fonda's Simon Fry, as seen in episodes such as "Badge for a Day," "Shadow of the Noose," and "Hang the Law," adds twists and nuances to the television Western genre's portrayal of the Western marshal, and is easily the equal of the characters he played in *Warlock* and *The Tin Star*. If not all the episodes of the series could live up to the high standard audiences expected from a Fonda production, we at least have Fonda to watch in those episodes of *The Deputy* he starred in all the way through—the equivalent of six full-length films.

And that's something to treasure, not dismiss.

CHAPTER SEVEN

The Deputy
Episode Guide

*T*he *Deputy* was produced by Top Gun Productions and MCA-TV for the NBC Television Network. The series ran from September 12, 1959 through September 16, 1961, including repeats. 76 episodes were shot in black & white on film. The series aired on Saturday nights at 9:00pm throughout its network run.

The major sponsors and agencies were The Kellogg Company through the Leo Burnett Company, Inc., and General Cigar Company (White Owl Cigars and Robert Burns Cigarillos) through Young & Rubicam, Inc.

Executive producers: William Frye, Henry Fonda (uncredited, through Top Gun); producer: Michel Kraike; created by: Roland Kibbee and Norman Lear; Music Score: Jack Marshall; Director of Photography: Ellsworth Fredericks, Ray Corey, William A. Sickner, Lionel Lindon; Art Direction: Martin Obzina, Russell Kimball, Arthur Lonergan; Editorial Supervisor: Richard G. Wray, David J. O'Connell; Film Editor: Patrick McCormack, James D. Ballas,

Douglas Stewart; Music Supervisor: Stanley Wilson; Sound: Corson Jowett, John K. Kean, Clarence E. Self; Makeup: Jack Barron; Set Decorator: William Tapp, John McCarthy, Carl Lawrence; Costume Supervisor: Vincent Dee; Hair Stylist: Florence Bush; Assistant Director: Ben Bishop; Story Editor: Finlay McDermid.

Series produced by Top Gun Productions; Filmed by Revue Productions, Inc.; Distributed by MCA Television Limited.

Cast: Henry Fonda (Chief Marshal Simon Fry); Allen Case (Deputy Marshal Clay McCord); Wallace Ford (Marshal Herk Lamson); Betty Lou Keim (Fran McCord); Read Morgan (Sergeant Hapgood Tasker).

Synopsis: The exploits of Chief Marshal Simon Fry, the marshal of the Arizona Territory, and his deputy, Clay McCord, in and around Silver City, Arizona, in 1880, as they struggle to keep the peace and maintain law and order.

The following episode guide includes information about all 76 episodes, including titles, writers, directors, and guest stars.

Each episode is also designated, with an explanation, as a "Fonda" or a "Non Fonda," the term used by the series producers in describing the involvement of the Simon Fry character in the story. The author has taken the liberty of expanding the definition to also include those episodes where the Fonda segments are more than mere cameos, even if he is not fully featured in that episode.

Author's notes on individual episodes are also included, and may refer to the episode itself or the series in general.

SEASON ONE,
September 12, 1959- September 17, 1961

Episode 1.1

Badge for a Day. September 12, 1959. Written by Roland Kibbee and Norman Lear. Directed by Don Medford. Produced by William Frye.

Guests stars: Robert J. Wilke (Ace Gentry), James Griffith (Ballard), Steven Ritch (Cowboy), Quentin Sondergaard (Tomick), and Earl Hansen (Stubber).

In the series pilot, Marshal Simon Fry is tracking the Ace Gentry gang and arrests two members secretly hauling supplies to the outlaws. Fry takes them to Silver City, where he tricks them into revealing the location of the gang's hideout, and then cons Silver City storeowner and top gun Clay McCord into joining him on an undercover mission to arrest the rest of the gang.

Category: FONDA. Simon Fry is seen throughout this episode, the first of his six major appearances in the season.

Notes: The first words we hear are part of Fry's narration: *"That was the Arizona territory in 1880, and I was its chief marshal."* This episode actually premiered in Canada on CBC- TV on September 10, 1959, two days before it aired in the United States; it was one of only two American Westerns to air in Canada that season. [237]

Episode 1.2

The Wild Wind. September 19, 1959. Written by N.B. Stone, Jr. Directed by David Butler. Produced by Michel Kraike.

Guests stars: Catherine McLeod (Charlotte Nelson), Joel Colin (Tommy Wilson), Richard Shannon (Bull Ward), John Ashley (Trooper Nelson), and Gary Vinson (Hi- Pockets).

Local teenagers in Silver City get mixed up with a newcomer to town, Bull Ward, described by Simon Fry as a "fence jumper." Ward murders a local sheep rancher and steals the sheep. Clay befriends one of the youths and entrusts him with a gold shipment. Clay and the boy's older sister are concerned that he's heading down the wrong path.

Category: NON FONDA. Simon is seen at the beginning of the episode trying to convince Clay to join him in nearby Saugus Valley to settle a water rights dispute. Simon also marvels at the sight of Clay selling a woman a pair of bloomers and at the price of "some new kind of fruit"—bananas for a dime apiece.

Notes: Allen Case told a reporter in 1960 that the series' focus on the family—the brother and sister, and the grandfather image represented by Wally Ford—was like "Father Knows Best in the West." [238]

Episode 1.3

Back to Glory. September 26, 1959. Repeated July 30, 1960. Written by Charles B. Smith. Directed by Felix Feist. Produced by Michel Kraike.

Guest stars: Marie Windsor (Angela), Frank De Kova (Cowan), Carol Leigh (Lilly), and Jack Lambert (Keever).

Clay and Marshal Lamson must catch a group of killers who murdered innocent settlers and raped two women. Fry rescued one of the women and rode off after the other, who had been kidnapped, only to fall ill. Lamson's experience as a lawman is needed to arrest the outlaws.

Category: FONDA. A Non Fonda episode by series standards, Fry is seen in two long sequences at the beginning of the episode, talking to the woman he rescued, and then at the end of the episode, congratulating Clay and Herk on a job well-done.

Notes: Upon hiring Wallace Ford for the role of Herk Lamson, Fonda said, "We've cut off some of that cascading white hair he usually has."[239]

Episode 1.4

Shadow of the Noose. October 3, 1959. Repeated August 6, 1960. Written by Roland Kibbee. Directed by Robert B. Sinclair. Produced by Michel Kraike.

Guests stars: Clu Gulager (Drifter), Denver Pyle (Akins), and John McKee (Sheriff Hollister).

In Oresburg, Fry arrests a drifter he knows killed a couple outside of town. A group of angry townspeople threaten to take the law into their own hands. Fry must hold off the lynch mob while transporting the man to Prescott via Silver City for trial. By stopping off in Silver City, Fry hopes to convince Clay to join him on the trail and help keep the lynch mob at bay.

Category: FONDA. Fry is seen throughout this episode, one of the best episodes of the series.

Notes: The episode is examined in detail in Chapter Five.

Episode 1.5

Powder Keg. October 10, 1959. Written by Ron Bishop and Wells Root. Directed by David Butler. Produced by Michel Kraike.

Guest stars: Read Morgan (Vince), Ben Bigelow (Jess), Onslow Stevens (Tom Deaver), and Christopher Dark (Hawk).

Herk Lamson and a deputy, Vince, must escort Tom Deaver to Prescott to stand trial on charges he is working with the Apaches "against his own kind." Clay also discovers that Deaver's son, an Apache, is in possession of enough gunpowder to blow out the doors of forts. Herk, Clay, and Vince work out a peace treaty and deliver the Deavers to Simon in Prescott. Simon tells Clay that it looks like the "storekeeper finally growed up to where he's thinkin' like a marshal's deputy."

Category: FONDA. Though a Non Fonda episode by series standards, Simon does appear in long sequences at the start of the episode (sending a telegram to Lamson from Prescott) and at the end of the episode as Herk and Clay bring the Deavers in, peace treaty in hand.

Notes: As the series started, Fonda said the producers were looking for another fellow to make a star out of. Five episodes in, Allen Case was on his way. Read Morgan, appearing here under his MCA contract, would join the series as Sgt. Tasker in the second episode of season two.

Episode 1.6

Like Father, -. October 17, 1959. Repeated July 23, 1960. Written by Jerry Sackheim. Directed by David Butler. Produced by Michel Kraike.

Guest Stars: Tom Laughlin (Jim Stanton), Paul Engle (Ted), Mickey Simpson (Gale Willow), Fred Beir (Brad Vantage), and James Westerfield (Chesley Vantage).

A gunman comes to Silver City seeking revenge against the new Silver City veterinarian, Brad Vantage. Clay discovers the two men were in a Kansas prison at the same time, and the gunman blames Vantage for a failed escape attempt. Ches Vantage, Brad's father, a reformed outlaw himself, had sent the boy away to be raised "right" by relatives, but the relatives were convinced that the boy would turn out bad because his father had been bad. Fran tries to stop the gunfight by telling Brad her own father died behind a gun and that there was a lot to live for. Clay has Brad arrested on a shoplifting charge before taking out the gunman himself.

Category: NON FONDA. Fry has a fight scene with the gunman in a Prescott saloon as the episode opens, but is not seen again. Simon's narration at the start of the episode discusses what he calls two kinds of law in the Arizona Territory—that for honest folks and that for those who believe in kill or be killed.

Notes: Director David Butler brought years of experience with him to the set; he had been a stage actor, silent film actor, Hollywood executive, and started directing films in 1927. The title of the episode as seen in the on-screen credit is "Like Father, -"

Episode 1.7

Proof of Guilt. October 24, 1959. Written by Melvin Levy. Directed by Arthur Lubin. Produced by Michel Kraike.

Guest stars: Roy Barcroft (Cooper), Harry Stephens (Joe Carey), Whitney Blake (Ellen Hart), and Mark Tapscott (Hart).

When the son of a reformed outlaw takes part in a gold robbery, the father decides to take the blame himself. Herk and Clay team up to stop the robberies and reunite the grandfather with his son's family.

Category: NON FONDA. Simon appears at the beginning of the episode, talking to an essayer about the gold robberies and Herk Lamson's age.

Notes: Director Arthur Lubin said he never viewed television as inferior to films, and of his television work in the 1950s, he added, "I gradually got in to television, I think all of us had to, to make a living, in between our feature pictures." [240]

Episode 1.8

The Johnny Shanks Story. October 31, 1959. Written by N.B. Stone, Jr. Directed by David Butler. Produced by Michel Kraike.

Guest stars: Skip Homeier (Johnny Shanks), Paul Campbell (Gib Kinman), Margo Lungreen (Athelia).

Three bounty hunters arrive in Silver City looking for con man Johnny Shanks. Fran convinces Clay to take a job as a guide for a group of settlers heading out of town so that he won't become involved in the trouble, but Shanks hooks up with the wagon train and Clay has to stop both him and the bounty hunters to keep the settlers safe.

Category: NON FONDA. Fonda appears at the start of the episode in a sequence in the McCord General Store.

Notes: Read Morgan said that between takes, Allen Case could often be seen on the telephone, tending to his other business interests. [241]

Episode 1.9

Focus of Doom. November 7, 1959. Repeated July 16, 1960. Written by Michel Kraike (story) and Sidney Michaels (teleplay). Directed by Arthur Lubin. Produced by Michel Kraike.

Guest stars: Eduard Franz (Wilk), Dennis Patrick (Regan), Vic Perrin (Madden), and Clarke Alexander (Barker).

Marshal Fry sends Sheriff Lamson away on a vacation when he fears that the assassin who has already killed three marshals in the territory is headed for Silver City. Simon sets himself up as the target, but keeps the plan to himself, leading Herk and Clay to believe that Herk is being let go. Simon, Clay, and Fran all confront the killer at the end.

Category: FONDA. Fonda is seen throughout the episode.

Notes: Writing in September, Cecil Smith of the *Los Angeles Times* said, "*The Deputy* seems to me to have lively qualities which set it apart from the usual western formula." [242]

Episode 1.10

The Big Four. November 14, 1959. Repeated August 20, 1960. Written by Kay Lenard and Jess Carneol. Directed by David Butler. Produced by Michel Kraike.

Guest stars: Henry Brandon (Johnny Ringo), Richard Bakalyan (Billy), Charles Fredericks (Curly Bill Brocius), and Gerald Milton (Ike Clanton).

When outlaw gangs band together, they bring a new form of crime to the Arizona Territory, prompting criticism of Simon's law enforcement efforts. Clay decides on his own to go undercover into the outlaw gang to try to learn their plans and alert Marshal Fry (via carrier pigeon). The outlaws include Billy the Kid, Johnny Ringo, Ike Clanton, and Curly Bill Brocious.

Category: NON FONDA. At the end of the episode, Simon tells Clay to make certain Fran knows that Clay got himself into trouble, without any help from the chief marshal.

Notes: This is an unusual episode of the series in that it uses actual historical figures in the storyline. The Writer's Presentation for the series suggested that historical figures could be used from time to time, but they rarely were.

Episode 1.11

The Next Bullet. November 28, 1959. Written by Kay Lenard and Jess Carneol. Directed by David Butler. Produced by Michel Kraike.

Guest stars: Brad Weston (Tom Clements), Jennifer Lea (Ann), and Walter Coy (Benson).

A note pinned to the chest of a murder victim says Herk Lamson will be the next victim. A recent murder trial seems to be what connects the murders and the threat, even as Clay and Fran defend a local man wrongfully accused of a crime he did not commit.

Category: NON FONDA. Simon pops up on a darkened street at night to counsel Clay about the situation.

Notes: Walter Coy was one of several guest stars in the series who had also appeared with Henry Fonda in *Warlock*.

Episode 1.12
The Deal. December 5, 1959. Repeated September 3, 1960. Written by Michel Kraike (story) and Herbert Purdom (teleplay). Directed by Herschel Daugherty. Produced by Michel Kraike.

Guest stars: Kelly Thordson (Hamish), Mel Welles (Jack Usher), David Halper (Ted), and Robert Osterloh (Quincannon).

Fran is kidnapped by outlaws who want to force Clay to help them steal a mining payroll. Simon and Clay mount a rescue mission after an intense argument in which Simon's strict law-and-order policies conflict with Clay's desire to rescue his sister unharmed.

Category: FONDA. Fonda is seen throughout the episode. Simon even spears an outlaw during the episode's climatic fistfight. At the end of the story, Simon calls it "a good day" because Fran was recovered safely and the outlaws held accountable.

Notes: That Fonda owned a large stake in the series was not unusual for the actor at this stage in his career. For example, he also owned 25% of the play *Two for the Seesaw*, in which he had invested $20,000 and had starred in during 1957- 58. [243]

Episode 1.13

Land Greed. December 12, 1959. Written by Katherine Albert and Dale Eunson. Directed by Robert B. Sinclair. Produced by Michel Kraike.

Guest stars: Vivian Vance (Emma Gant), Frank Albertson (Nick Harper), Grace Albertson (Mrs. Harper), and Robin Riley (Billy).

Widow Emma Gant tries to get the law's help when she says she and her son are being forced off their land by large ranch owners. She publicly calls out rancher Nick Harper during a Sunday church service. Gant later accuses Harper of rustling her cattle, but Harper denies it.

Category: NON FONDA. Simon has a conversation with Clay in his office in Prescott. He asks Clay to watch over Ms. Gant as a private citizen so that it doesn't look like the law is taking one side over the other.

Notes: The episode is highlighted by the television dramatic debut of Vivian Vance, well known for her role as Ethel Mertz on *I Love Lucy*. Vance was nervous about the role, after years of comedy on television, saying, "The woman I play is a strong individualist who rides horses and drives buggies. It's given me a new lease on life." [244]

Episode 1.14

Man of Peace. December 19, 1959. Written by Roland Kibbee (story) and Herbert Purdom (teleplay). Directed by Frank Arrigo. Produced by Michel Kraike.

Guest stars: Edgar Buchanan (Isbel), Robert Warwick (Chief Magnus), Robert Sampson (Micah), Arthur Kendall (Mordecai), and Dennis Cross (Chivas).

Simon sends for the Army when Apache Indians steal some rifles. But Clay tries to head off further hostilities by talking to the Apaches directly. Clay discovers that the real trouble is being caused by a father and his sons.

Category: NON FONDA. Fonda is seen mostly at the beginning of this episode, a fine showcase for Allen Case, courtesy of series creator Roland Kibbee's story idea and Herb Purdom's teleplay. The title is direct reference to Kibbee's idea for the character of Clay McCord.

Notes: In a 1960 interview, Allen Case said the portrayal of Indians in television westerns was a pet peeve of his. "They always make them look stupid. And all TV Indians wear Apache wigs even if they're supposed to be Sioux, Comanche, or Navajos. And they're all made to look like actors, even the few real Indians who work. Then the dialogue is always the same—'You Great White Father.' And the white man talks back in the same way." [245]

Episode 1.15

The Orphans. December 26, 1959. Written by Katherine Albert and Dale Eunson. Directed by Frederick Stephani. Produced by Michel Kraike.

Guest stars: Lane Bradford (Finley), Karl Lukas (Luke Dillon), Fred Sherman (Parson Leeds), and Dennis Rush (Timmy).

The citizens of Silver City try to help three orphans whose parents have been viciously murdered. Simon stages a raffle to help raise money for the children but also to lure in the killers. Simon's idea is to fix the raffle, with Clay as the winner, as a way to capture the killers.

Category: NON FONDA. Simon appears briefly on horseback at the beginning of the episode, and then in an extended sequence with Herk Lamson, planning the raffle as a way to set Clay up as bait for the outlaws.

Notes: Wallace Ford dons a Santa Claus suit in his role as Marshal Herk Lamson.

Episode 1.16

Backfire. January 2, 1960. Written by Wilton Schiller. Directed by James Hogan. Produced by Michel Kraike.

Guest stars: Paula Raymond (Peg Marlowe), Charles Cooper (Con Marlowe), Robert Carson (Kin Maxwell), and Bob Steele (Fred Sooley).

Herk Lamson defends himself against an outlaw but has to shoot the man in the back, and loses the respect of some Silver City residents in the process. Adding to Herk's troubles is the outlaw's widow, who has hired two gunmen to avenge her husband's death.

Category: NON FONDA. Simon appears briefly, but the episode is a showcase for Allen Case as Clay and Wally Ford as Herk Lamson.

Notes: Speaking with a reporter as the show premiered the previous September, Fonda said, "I appear in a few scenes to help establish the story, then leave the rest to Allen." The pattern was well-established by episode sixteen. [246]

Episode 1.17

Hang the Law. January 9, 1960. Written by Herbert Purdom. Directed by Robert B. Sinclair. Produced by Michel Kraike.

Guest stars: Martha Hyer (Joy Cartwright), Lillian Bronson (Blanche), Willard Sage (Rev. Cartwright), Grant Richards (Frank Ivy), and Robert Foulk (Easter).

Simon tries to prove Clay innocent of a trumped-up murder charge in a border town. To do so he must romance a clergyman's sister and survive verbal jousts with the town's leading citizen and matriarch, Blanche Niles.

Category: FONDA. One of the first season's highlights and indeed one of the highlights of the series, this episode features a strong script by veteran western writer Herb Purdom, fine direction from Bob Sinclair, and top-notch guest stars, including Martha Hyer and Lillian Bronson. Martha Hyer sings in this episode, and there is a wonderful scene in which Lillian Bronson, as Blanche, pulls a gun on Simon and forces him to give up his weapon.

Notes: The working title for this episode, detailed in Chapter Five, was "Framed."

Episode 1.18

Silent Gun. January 23, 1960. Written by Rik Vollaerts. Directed by Sidney Lanfield. Produced by Michel Kraike.

Guest stars: Marcia Henderson (Marion Whelan), Dean Fredericks (Pete Clemson), Howard Wright (Stoner), and Grandon Rhodes (Mayor).

A stranger comes to Silver City and immediately starts to gun down residents in fair fights. Only a few citizens of Silver City know the reason behind his visit, including local school teacher Marion Whelan, who was once engaged to the man. The stranger must let his gun do his talking because he was left mute by a mob's rope ten years before. He has come to Silver City looking for revenge.

Category: NON FONDA. Simon appears in the middle of the episode to tell Clay about the background of the gunslinger. Simon also appears in a flashback sequence in which we learn that he saved the gunslinger from the hanging ten years before.

Notes: Allen Case said he didn't like the way women were often portrayed on television westerns. He said, "They're either maudlin or broken down, carrying pots and pans around, or they're just out and out bad women. There's no in-between. That's plain idiotic." [247]

Episode 1.19

The Hidden Motive. January 30, 1960. Written by Michel Kraike (story) and Jess Carneol and Kay Lenard (teleplay). Directed by Sidney Lanfield. Fonda segments directed by Robert B. Sinclair, uncredited. Produced by Michel Kraike.

Guest stars: Roxanne Berard (Louise Spencer)), Jeremy Slate (Red Dawson), Paul Sheriff (Len Dawson), and Charlie Briggs (Bill Dawson).

Guilt-ridden, Clay offers his services as handyman to a gunman's widow after he is forced to kill the man in a gunfight. She misunderstands his intentions, however. Clay travels to Prescott to talk to Simon and sort out his feelings about the killing. Clay tries to find out what the dead man's motives were.

Category: NON FONDA. Simon is seen getting a haircut, a sight not common among television's lawmen. Simon also reveals that he has a cast on his foot—a clever, if inevitable, way to keep Simon out of a story.

Notes: One of the reasons NBC placed this series on Saturday was because Perry Como and his variety show had moved to Wednesday night.

Episode 1.20

Lawman's Blood. February 6, 1960. Written by Charles B. Smith. Directed by John Brahm. Produced by Michel Kraike.

Guest stars: Willis Bouchey (Doc Landy), Phillip Pine (Jack Burch), Ronnie Burns (Morgan Burch).

Clay must rescue Doc Landy, the Silver City physician, who has been kidnapped and taken to treat an outlaw wounded by Simon Fry.

Category: NON FONDA. Fonda appears at the beginning of the episode, as Simon and a posse save a wagon train under attack by white men disguised as Indians.

Notes: This episode features a fine turn by character actor Willis Bouchy as Doc Landy, marking the first appearance of the character, later played regularly by Addison Richards. Prior to this episode, the only physician referred to in Silver City had been Doc Miller, but we are told in this episode that he is in the east.

Episode 1.21

The Return of Simon Fry. February 13, 1960. Repeated August 13, 1960. Written by Terence Maples. Directed by Arthur Lubin. Produced by Michel Kraike.

Guest stars: Stacy Keach, Sr. (Vic Rufus), Larry Johns (Silas Jones), Hugh Sanders (Jake Carter), Peter Mamakos (Jubba), and Frank Richards (Kip).

After as assassination attempt on him fails, Simon plays dead and goes undercover to discover who tried to have him killed and why. Clay, Fran, and Herk travel to Prescott to attend the funeral, and learn that Simon is still alive. Clay and Herk help Simon learn the truth.

Category: FONDA. In fact, the episode is a fine display not only for Fonda but for all the members of the regular cast as the characters react personally to the news that Simon is dead. This is, unfortunately, the sixth and last full appearance by Henry Fonda during the series' first season.

Notes: It was announced the week prior to this telecast that both Betty Lou Keim and Wallace Ford's characters would depart the series by April. [248]

Episode 1.22

Queen Bea. February 20, 1960. Written by Herbert Purdom. Directed by Herschel Daugherty. Fonda segment directed by Robert B. Sinclair, uncredited. Produced by Michel Kraike.

Guest stars: Phyllis Avery (Beatrice Vale), Kim Spaulding (Briscoe), and Paul Dubov (Fletcher).

Protection racketeers move into Silver City, hoping to ruin the local merchants and pave the way for a chain of stores. Herk, Clay, and Fran fight off the racketeers and their leader, Beatrice Vale.

Category: NON FONDA. Simon is seen at the beginning of the episode, riding into Silver City, asleep on his horse. He's also seen hatching a plan with Herk to get Clay involved in breaking up the protection rackets.

Notes: There is an insightful exchange in this episode between Herk and Fran. The marshal orders Fran not to join the fight, but she not only ignores him, she arms herself with a rifle, and wrestles Beatrice Vale to the floor.

Episode 1.23

The Two Faces of Bob Claxton. February 27, 1960. Written by Charles O'Neal. Directed by David Butler. Fonda segment directed by Robert B. Sinclair, uncredited. Produced by Michel Kraike.

Guest stars: Robert Montgomery, Jr. (Bob Claxton), Bob Hopkins (Mike Claxton), Ron Soble (Soloman Claxton), Johnny Seven (Pete Claxton), and Rusty Lane (Judge Jones).

Clay and Fran try to rehabilitate a teenager wounded while taking part in a failed bank robbery. The boy only pretends to go along, however, and rejoins his brothers when they arrive in Silver City to free him. His refusal to change his life costs Bob Claxton his life.

Category: NON FONDA. Simon appears long enough to convince Fran that it would be a good idea for the young Claxton boy to stay with the McCords. Fonda's segment, totaling about six pages of script, was shot October 9, 1959.

Notes: The working title for this episode was "The Kid." This episode, with its concentration on the McCords, and their efforts to help the young man, is an example of what the series lost when Betty Lou Keim left the series.

Episode 1.24

Lady with a Mission. March 5, 1960. Written by Charles B. Smith. Directed by Sidney Lanfield. Produced by Michel Kraike.

Guest stars: Jan Clayton (Agatha Stone), Beverly Allison (Gloria Jennings), Carleton Young (Sam Hodges), Tod Griffin (Tinney), and James Lanphier (Sloan).

A suffragette arrives in Silver City and prompts outrage from the community's male citizens. Fran joins the right to vote movement against Clay's wishes.

Category: NON FONDA. Simon is seen only at the beginning of the episode in Prescott, pledging law enforcement help for the women's suffrage movement, though the women doubt his sincerity.

Notes: In 1960, Allen Case told a reporter, "Basically, I'm a business-man with some kind of an urge to act." [249]

Episode 1.25

The Border Between. March 12, 1960. Written by Hal Biller and Austin Kalish. Directed by Frank Arrigo. Produced by Michel Kraike.

Guest stars: Anna Kashfi (Felipa), Leo Gordon (Evan Sloat), Laurie Mitchell (Lorrie), Brett Pearson (Powell), and Steve Mitchell (Zimmler).

A landowner holding Simon and Clay hostage makes a deal with his prisoners—Clay can save their lives if he brings back the man's daughter, who has eloped.

Category: NON FONDA. As the series produced more episodes, some of the contrivances used to explain Simon's absences worked better than others. In this case, Clay and Simon are taken prisoner and the audience sees only Clay, and not Simon, questioned by the landowner. Clay is tied to a post and whipped in this episode.

Notes: Jack Marshall's theme from the series was included in 2002 as part of a CD released by the Laurie Johnson Orchestra called "The Avengers and Other Top 60s TV Themes."

Episode 1.26

Final Payment. March 19, 1960. Written by Charles R. Marion. Directed by Frank Arrigo. Fonda segment directed by Robert B. Sinclair, uncredited. Produced by Michel Kraike.

Guest stars: Gerald Mohr (Dustin Groat), Kevin Hagen (Kemmer), Mari Aldon (Priscilla Grant), Charles Seel (Doc Miller).

Groat, a man confined to a wheelchair, is out for vengeance against Clay and Fran because he blames their father, Luke McCord, for his paralysis. Groat buys the note on Clay's store from the bank and starts proceedings to put the McCords out of business.

Category: NON FONDA. Fonda appears in one scene in the middle of the first act, when Clay rides out on the trail to tell Simon he's not needed in Prescott. Fonda's segment was shot on October 12, 1959.

Notes: The working title for this episode was "The Tycoon." Doc Miller reappears, having been "back east" in the episode "Lawman's Blood." Eventually, Doc Landy becomes the permanent recurring physician character in the series.

Episode 1.27

Dark Reward. March 26, 1960. Repeated August 27, 1960. Written by Marianne Mosner. Directed by Louis King. Fonda segment directed by Robert B. Sinclair, uncredited. Produced by Michel Kraike.

Guest stars: John Dennis (Hawkins), Jean Willes (Rosie), Richard Garland (Matt Ross), Frances Morris (Mrs. Carter).

Clay helps Herk Lamson put an end to a series of bank robberies. Complicating matters is a bankers association, which has put up a reward for dead thieves.

Category: NON FONDA. Fonda as Simon Fry does have an important scene in Herk Lamson's office arguing with a banker about the reward being offered.

Notes: Allen Case and Henry Fonda both have voice-overs in this episode. The character of Fran McCord is mentioned as being away in Bisby, a town Simon Fry often traveled to, as well.

Episode 1.28

Marked for Bounty. April 2, 1960. Written by William Yagemann. Directed by Sidney Lanfield. Fonda segment directed by Robert B. Sinclair, uncredited. Produced by Michel Kraike.

Guest stars: Regis Toomey (Warden Jess Martin), Alan Baxter (Mort Harch), Ron Hayes (Ralph Jenson), Edward Earle (Judge Jenson), Charles Seel (Doc Miller), Vito Scotti (Jose), and Raymond Hatton (Pete).

Ralph Jenson, a convict who was allowed by a warden to escape from prison to visit his dying father, a retired judge, is stalked by a bounty hunter.

Category: NON FONDA. Simon is seen talking to the warden at the beginning of the episode. Fonda's segment was shot on October 12, 1959; the shots of Simon riding are stock footage shot earlier that summer. The length of Fonda' segment is fairly typical for one of these appearances, about five script pages.

Notes: Jack Marshall's compositions for the series included "The Deputy Theme," "The Deputy Chase Theme" and "Arizona Rag." [250]

Episode 1.29

The Truly Yours. April 9, 1960. Repeated September 10, 1960. Written by Montgomery Pittman (story, teleplay) and Herbert Purdom (teleplay). Directed by David Butler.

Guest stars: James Coburn (Coffer), Adeline Pedroza (Juanita), Anthony Caruso (Fife), Miriam Colon (Cita), Mike Read (Faney), and Joe Dominguez (Pepe).

The series' transitional episode in terms of format, "The Truly Yours" depicts the burning of the McCords' general store and Clay's decision to become a full-time deputy marshal. His first job is to hunt down those who committed the crime.

Category: NON FONDA. Simon Fry is in town long enough to ask about Fran and Brandy (back east with relatives) and to tell Clay that Herk Lamson will retire (the outlaws who burned the store shattered Herk's arm).

Notes: The series adjusts its format with a fine guest cast—James Coburn and Anthony Caruso among them-- and a story from two veteran western hands, Monty Pittman and Herb Purdom.

Episode 1.30

A Time to Sow. April 23, 1960. Written by Kay Lenard and Jess Carneol. Directed by Louis King. Produced by Michel Kraike.

Guest stars: Richard Crenna (Andy Willis), Frank Ferguson (Tom McCullough), Coleen Gray (Lucy Willis), Howard J. Negley (Hank Bridges), and Dick Rich (Harris).

Clay is on the lookout for a hired killer, not suspecting—at first-- that young and friendly family man Andy Willis could be the person he's looking for. Willis has been hired by a cattleman feuding with a neighbor, but even Willis' wife does not know that her husband is a hired killer.

Category: NON FONDA. Simon appears at the beginning and the end of the episode, counseling Clay about the measures even honest citizens might resort to when desperate.

Notes: Henry Fonda did take every opportunity to cast promising young actors whenever possible. Here the actor is Richard Crenna, taking a timeout from *The Real McCoys*.

Episode 1.31

The Last Gunfight. April 30, 1960. Repeated September 17, 1960. Written by Richard Carr (story) and Charles B. Smith (teleplay). Directed by Sidney Lanfield. Produced by Michel Kraike.

Guest stars: Charles McGraw (Johnny Dean), Robert Redford (Burt Johnson), Paul Clark (David Crawford), Monica Lewis (Helen Ivers), Perry Ivins (Haskins), and Phil Tully (Charlie).

Two young gunfighters argue over the chance to goad a reformed gunfighter into a duel, believing they will gain a reputation and prominence. Johnny Deane, the reformed outlaw, tries to talk them out of it and urges them to move on. The gunfighters decide the only way to determine who gets to duel Deane is to first duel each other, Deane runs between the two and is gunned down. Clay decides to keep the identity of the killer a secret so that neither can profit from Deane's sacrifice.

Category: NON FONDA. Simon appears only at the beginning and close of the episode, which does offer a wonderful closing narration by Henry Fonda. It is one of the better NON FONDAS of the series.

Notes: This episode, utilizing one of the oldest stand-by plots in the Western, is redeemed by strong performances from a good cast, including veteran performer Charles McGraw and a young Robert Redford. This episode is incorrectly cited in several sources as Redford's television debut. Redford had appeared in at least three other television series (*Maverick, Hallmark Hall of Fame,* and *Rescue 8*) before this episode aired in late April.

Episode 1.32

The Chain of Action. May 7, 1960. Written by Lester Fuller. Directed by Sidney Lanfield. Produced by Michel Kraike.

Guest stars: Lee Paterson (Lig Schofield), Bek Nelson (Claudia), Francis DeSales (Porter), and Will J. Wright (Delaney).

Condemned to die, a robber refuses to say where he hid stolen money, despite the fact that the money was intended to save a young boy from blindness.

Category: NON FONDA. Simon appears in three short segments in the episode, as he and Clay try to force an outlaw to reveal where stolen money was hidden. Clay asks Simon to delay the outlaw's hanging until they know where the money is.

Notes: The paperback tie-in to the series was Dell publication titled simply "The Deputy" and written by Roe Richmond. The 1960 release sold for 35 cents. The story concerned a gunslinger, Johnny Breed, who had sworn revenge against Simon Fry for sending him away to Yuma prison. The story was published again in 1986 by Bantam as "The Saga of Simon Fry."

Episode 1.33

Lucifer Urge. May 14, 1960. Written by Ellis Kadison. Directed by Sidney Lanfield. Produced by Michel Kraike.

Guest stars: George Tobias (Barney Wagner), Ralph Moody (Walt Conroy), James Bell (Rob Stebbins), Nancy Valentine (Alva Wagner), and Vito Scotti (Jose).

Barney Wagner, the man who put the last bullet into Clay's father, arrives in Silver City demanding that Clay serve legal notices to evict local ranchers off their property.

Category: NON FONDA. Simon appears in a sequence with Clay in the first act and then again in the last scene convincing a circuit judge to bypass Silver City for an additional week. This will give ranchers time enough to properly register their land claims and avoid eviction by Barney Wagner.

Notes: What on the surface would appear to be a compelling story for Clay tends to fall flat because of the performance of George Tobias as Wagner. A character that is supposed to be threatening instead comes across as the opposite. Allen Case does have a revealing line of dialogue prior to the episode's decisive gun battle, however: "If you won't take it for boastin', I'm faster than my father ever was." [251]

Episode 1.34

Palace of Chance. May 21, 1960. Written by Charles B. Smith. Directed by Sidney Lanfield. Produced by Michel Kraike.

Guest stars: Karen Steele (Julie Grant), Steve Brodie (Fischer), Lee Van Cleef (Cherokee Kid), Vito Scotti (Jose), and Dennis Cross (George Reed).

Despite the protests of local businessmen, Clay refuses to shut down a new gambling hall in Silver City in hopes that it will lure in a wanted man, whose girlfriend works there.

Category: NON FONDA.

Notes: Another good first-season guest star list in this episode, including Karen Steele, Lee Van Cleef, Steve Brodie, and Vito Scotti in his third appearance as Jose (he would make six appearances in the first season, filling in the gap after the departure of Betty Lou Keim and Wallace Ford).

Episode 1.35

The X Game. May 28, 1960. Written by Herbert Purdom. Directed by David Butler. Produced by Michel Kraike.

Guest stars: John Hoyt (Hap Allison), Don Gordon (Queed), Howard Wendell (Webb), Tom McKee (Coyle), Carlos Rivera (Huerta), and Edward Foster (Tomaso).

An illiterate farmer is swindled by dishonest businessmen—he puts his X on a piece of paper and promptly signs away his land. It's a con that's been sweeping across the territory and Clay vows to stop it.

Category: NON FONDA. Simon is seen in one scene telling Clay there isn't much the law can do to help the farmer.

Notes: Theme composer Jack Marshall's 1960 album "The Marshall Swings!" is described on the album cover as "Jack Marshall swings songs of the wide open spaces."

Episode 1.36

The Standoff. June 11, 1960. Written by Louis Paul (story) and Ellis Kadison (teleplay). Directed by David Butler. Produced by Michel Kraike.

Guest stars: Alan Hale Jr. (Frank Angle), Ann McCrea (Helen Swayde), Vito Scotti (Jose), Addison Richards (Doc Landy).

Simon Fry is bushwhacked by an escaped criminal and Clay decides to pick up the pursuit. He engages in a battle of wills with the criminal before the man surrenders.

Category: NON FONDA. Simon is seen on horseback and then limping into Clay's office, but the episode belongs to Allen Case once Clay goes after the outlaw himself.

Notes: Allen Case' 1960 Columbia album release, "The Deputy Sings," featured an orchestra under the direction of Frank DeVol.

Episode 1.37

Trail of Darkness. June 18, 1960. Written by Rik Vollaerts. Directed by Sidney Lanfield. Produced by Michel Kraike.

Guest stars: Donald Woods (Douglas Brainard), Gregg Palmer (Tully), Clu Gulager (Sanford), Addison Richards (Doc Landy), and Vito Scotti (Jose).

Doug Brainard sends two gunmen to either free or kill a member of his gang captured by Clay McCord and guarded by Simon Fry. The outlaw masks his identity from the gang and Silver City residents by wearing a bag over his head. Clay, kidnapped and beaten, subsequently retraces his steps to the gang's hideout by listening to sounds along the trail.

Category: NON FONDA. Fonda's scenes in this episode are a glaring example of end of the first season continuity errors. Simon's sideburns are extremely dark, when they had been graying in previous episodes.

Notes: This is one of several episodes in which it is mentioned that Clay is trying to save money to rebuild the McCord General Store. Simon often found a way to give reward money to someone other than Clay.

Episode 1.38

The Choice. June 25, 1960. Written by Saul Schwartz (story, teleplay) and Lester Fuller (teleplay). Directed by David Butler. Produced by Michel Kraike.

Guest stars: Vince Edwards (Dory Matson), Rex Holman (Ben Sutton), Chris Alcaide (Fred Tanner), Vitto Scotti (Jose), Phil Tully (Charlie), and Addison Richards (Doc Landy).

A story of second chances, this fine episode stars Vince Edwards as an ex-convict who returns to Silver City. Dory Matson runs into trouble from local residents, who won't forget his past. Simon even orders Clay to run Matson out of Silver City as a vagrant if he can't find a job. Doc Landy brings Matson on as a medical assistant after learning he worked in the prison ward for five years and becomes determined to help Matson realize his dream of becoming a doctor.

Category: NON FONDA. Simon and Clay have an intense discussion in the office as Simon orders Clay to get Dory Matson out of town.

Notes: Actor Vince Edwards said in a 1962 interview that Henry Fonda's casting of him in this episode helped him land the role for which he is best remembered, *Ben Casey*. Producer Michael Kraike saw how well Edwards fit into the medical role and tried to convince Revue to spin this episode off into a series of its own.[252] Also in this episode, Addison Richards, who took over the role of Doc Landy from Willis Bouchy, appears for the third time.

Episode 1.39

Ma Mack. July 9, 1960. Written by Rod Peterson. Directed by Robert B. Sinclair. Produced by Michel Kraike.

Guest stars: Nina Varela (Ma Mack), Douglas Kennedy (Bates), Gregory Walcott (Reece), Ron Brogan (Taylor), Ralph Neff (Bailey), and Jack Hogan (Abner).

Ma Mack, who claims to be an old friend of Luke McCord, arrives in Silver City and asks Clay's help in finding her son. Clay agrees, without knowing the real reason behind her search—the man she's searching for is her stepson, and she intends to kill him.

Category: NON FONDA. Simon appears early in the episode, talking to the lawman who is tracking Ma Mack. Simon is trying on a pair of boots he bought from Clay, but the boots don't feel right.

Notes: This first-run episode was originally produced to air much earlier in the season, and was shown here obviously out of sequence, as both Fran McCord and Herk Lamson appear in the story.

SEASON TWO
September 24, 1960- September 16, 1961

Episode 2.1
The Deadly Breed. September 24, 1960. Repeated June 3, 1961. Written by: William Yagemann. Directed by Virgil W. Vogel. Produced by Michel Kraike.

Guest stars: Susan Oliver (Julie), Lyle Bettger (Aces Thompson), Francis DeSales (Mattson), and Robert P. Lieb (Baker).

Simon takes an unusual interest in a pair of swindlers in Silver City, a father and his daughter. Clay can't understand why until he realizes that Simon once had a romantic interest in the girl's mother. Simon is determined to pry the young woman away from her father and give her a chance at a better life.

Category: FONDA. Fonda appears throughout the episode, which also features welcome guest turns from two top-notch performers, Susan Oliver and Lyle Bettger.

Notes: Composer Jack Marshall's western music was released on at least four albums: *Channel West!* by Johnny Gregory and his Orchestra (Columbia): *Hit Instrumentals from TV Westerns* by Al Caiola (United Artists); *Double Impact* by Buddy Morrow (Madrid RCA); and *Swingin' West* by Marty Gold (RCA Victor).

Episode 2.2

Meet Sergeant Tasker. October 1, 1960. Written by Richard N. Morgan. Directed by Reginald Le Borg. Produced by Michel Kraike.

Guest stars: Joan O'Brien (Emily Price), Richard Cutting (Gus), Phil Tully (Charlie), and Rayford Barnes (Charlie).

This episode introduces a new recurring character, Sergeant Hapgood Tasker, a Cavalry supply officer. Simon and Clay have to step in to prevent him from using force when he is victimized by thieves. Tasker's Army money is stolen by a dance hall girl.

Category: FONDA. Year two is off to a good start for Fonda fans, as the actor makes full appearances in the first two episodes of the season.

Notes: Director Reginald Le Borg, asked about working with Henry Fonda on this episode, said, "He practically walked through it. I had to give him one direction at a time. He lay down to sleep, and I said, 'Henry, when you sleep, take off your hat and put it over your head.' And he did it." Le Borg described working on this series and others as setting up the camera, "trying to get finished, and do the dialogue right." [253]

Episode 2.3

The Jason Harris Story. October 8, 1960. Repeated June 17, 1961. Written by Charles B. Smith. Directed by Tay Garnett. Produced by Michel Kraike.

Guest stars: Jeff Morrow (Harris), Dianne Foster (Laurie Harris), Myron Healey (Johnny Dustin), and Robert J. Stevenson (Morgan).

Simon, Clay, and Sgt. Tasker investigate troubling evidence that would appear to implicate Marshal Jason Harris in a series of robberies of gold shipments. The real culprit turns out to be Harris' wife.

Category: FONDA. Simon appears throughout the episode, at one point telling Sarge that rough tactics wouldn't be needed in the interrogation of Marshal Harris.

Notes: Read Morgan said that Henry Fonda was serious about his work and that "he ruled that place in his own quiet way." [254]

Episode 2.4

The Fatal Urge. October 15, 1960. Written by Joseph Carter. Directed by Tay Garnett. Produced by Michel Kraike.

Guest stars: Kathleen Crowley (Martha Jackson), Tony Young (Tweed Younger), Ron Starr (Phil Jackson), Argentina Brunetti (Evita), and Addison Richards (Doc Landy).

Clay suspects a wealthy man's nephew was involved in the man's death during a robbery attempt, but the nephew's sister refuses to believe it.

Category: NON FONDA. Fonda's narration is included, but Simon doesn't arrive until the final two minutes of the episode, when he shares a laugh in the saloon with Clay.

Notes: Years later, speaking of his own experience on a television series, James Stewart said, "Henry had also done well—better than I did—with a series called *The Deputy*." [255]

Episode 2.5

Mother and Son. October 29, 1960. Repeated July 8, 1961. Written by Charles R. Marion. Directed by Louis King. Produced by Michel Kraike.

Guest stars: James Franciscus (William Stanhope), Josephine Hutchinson (Mrs. Stanhope), Arthur Kendall (Deek House), Robert Karnes (Sam Nelson), Pitt Herbert (Clerk), Scotty Morrow (Phillip), and Joe Yrigoyen (Driver).

Simon arrests the outlaw William Stanhope and puts him in the Silver City jail to await transport to Prescott for trial, but then learns the man's mother has arrived in Silver City to see her son. When Simon discovers not only that she knows nothing of her son's criminal activities, but that she has only a short time to live, he and Clay decide they will allow Stanhope to spend time with his mother before she leaves town. The outlaw's time with his mother helps him to see the error of his ways and he helps the lawmen capture the gang he was running with.

Category: FONDA. Fonda shares some especially poignant scenes with character actress Josephine Hutchinson as Mrs. Stanhope.

Notes: James Franciscus was another in a series of impressive guest stars on the series. He is fondly remembered by television fans for his regular roles in a host of series, including *Naked City, The Investigators, Mr. Novak, Doc Elliot,* and *Hunter.*

Episode 2.6

Bitter Root. November 5, 1960. Written by Kay Lenard and Jess Carneol. Directed by Louis King. Produced by Michel Kraike.

Guest stars: Virginia Gregg (Hester Macklin), Don Megowan (Tim Brandon), Zon Murray (Joe Foss), and Paul Sorenson (Will Terry).

Simon, Clay, and Sgt. Tasker chase a trio of outlaws, led by the wounded Tim Brandon, into a remote area. Unsure which direction the outlaws went, the team splits up, with Simon riding one way and Clay and Tasker following another possible route. They catch up to Brandon at Bitter Root Springs watering hole, a cabin owned by Hester Macklin, who is hiding the killer. Macklin has been alone for years and hopes her company and the money she has made charging travelers for food and water will convince Brandon to stay with her. Clay and Tasker come to her defense when Brandon's gang returns.

Category: NON FONDA. Simon disappears for the episode after the team splits up to search, until he reappears again at the end for a conversation with Hester at the cabin.

Notes: Virginia Gregg was one of the great actresses from the age of network radio, playing character roles in hundreds of radio series episodes before branching out into film and television.

Episode 2.7

The Higher Law. November 12, 1960. Written by William Nash (story) and Charles B. Smith (teleplay). Directed by Tay Garnett. Produced by Michel Kraike.

Guest stars: John Larch (Jack Rivers), H.M. Wynant (Black Wing), Lewis Martin (Judge Wilkins), and Addison Richards (Doc Landy).

Clay and Sgt. Tasker try to prevent bloodshed when an Indian named Blackwing is shot and vows revenge. Problem: Blackwing refuses to tell them who the gunman was.

Category: NON FONDA. Fry is seen at the beginning of the episode rescuing a pony and then talking with Clay. Fonda does narrate the episode.

Notes: In the early 1970s, Henry Fonda said to John Wayne, while urging him to try a television series, "Duke, I wish I had waited until I was a little older before I did *The Deputy* because my movie career wasn't floundering back then." [256]

Episode 2.8

Passage to New Orleans. November 19, 1960. Repeated July 15, 1961. Written by Rik Vollaerts. Produced by Michel Kraike.

Guest stars: Patrice Wymore (Lucy Balance), George Douglas (Captain), Saul Gorss (Steward), Carl Benton Reid (Samuel Forceman), and Harvey Dunn (Sleepy Man).

A change-of-pace episode that takes place far away from Silver City and the Arizona Territory. Simon and Clay are onboard a riverboat, escorting murder witness Lucy Ballance to New Orleans, where she is to appear at a trial. Both lawmen romance Lucy as hired guns try to kill her to prevent her from testifying.

Category: FONDA. Simon not only romances the murder witness but gets involved in fisticuffs aboard ship, as well.

Notes: Read Morgan does not appear in this episode, one of only three in the second season in which Sgt. Tasker is not seen; the others are "The Deadly Breed" and "Sally Tornado."

Episode 2.9

The World Against Me. November 26, 1960. Written by Hal Biller and Austin Kalish. Directed by David Butler. Produced by Michel Kraike.

Guest stars: Dennis Joel (Tommy White), Henry Rowland (Brewer), Joseph Bassett (Boyd), Harry Clexx (Amos), and Fred Kruger (Grisby).

Outlaws are after Timmy White, a young boy who not only witnessed his grandfather's murder but knows the secret location of his grandfather's gold mine. Clay and Sgt. Tasker must protect the boy and bring the killers to justice.

Category: NON FONDA. Simon walks in on Sarge and Clay as they give the boy a bath.

Notes: It has often been written that Henry Fonda narrated every episode of the series. He did not. This episode includes a brief voice-over narration by Allen Case, but not Fonda.

Episode 2.10

Sally Tornado. December 3, 1960. Written by Charles B. Smith. Directed by Louis King. Produced by Michel Kraike.

Guest stars: Fay Spain (Sally), William Fawcett (Jipsom), Don O'Kelly (Hunter).

Simon arrests one of the territory's most dangerous criminals, Sally Tornado, a convicted murderer on the run. He asks Clay to escort Sally to Yuma so that the death sentence by hanging can be carried out. Simon warns Clay that she will try almost anything to regain her freedom.

Category: NON FONDA. Simon arrests Sally at the beginning of the episode by wrestling her and then tossing her onto a hotel room bed. At the end of the episode, we learn that Simon had asked that Sally's sentence be reduced from death to life in prison.

Notes: This episode is sometimes referred to under an alternate title, "Lady for a Hanging."

Episode 2.11

Three Brothers. December 10, 1960. Repeated July 22, 1961. Written by Peggy Shaw and Lou Shaw. Directed by Sidney Lanfield. Produced by Michel Kraike.

Guest stars: Cathy Case (Martha Towers), Jack Ging (Jay Bennett), Lew Gallo (Frank Bennett), Buzz Martin (Gary Bennett), Carmen Phillips (Suzy), Minga Mitchell (Terry Vance).

Simon must solve a confusing murder mystery and a series of bank robberies in this episode, which finds him also criticizing Clay and Sarge for not moving fast enough to solve the crimes.

Category: FONDA. Simon is seen throughout this episode, and grumpier than usual.

Notes: Authors Christopher Wicking and Tise Vahimagi, who wrote a book on American television directors, said that even though Lanfield directed his share of Westerns on television, "He didn't have dirty enough fingernails to bring any bite to westerns." [257]

Episode 2.12

Day of Fear. December 17, 1960. Repeated July 29, 1960. Written by Clark E. Reynolds. Directed by Tay Garnett. Produced by Michel Kraike.

Guest stars: Mary Tyler Moore (Amy Collins), Tyler McVey (Stu Collins), Robert Osterloh (Sam Nathan), Anne Barton (Gail Nathan), and Addison Richards (Doc Landy).

Simon must quarantine Silver City when rumor spreads that Clay has brought a possible smallpox victim to town.

Category: FONDA.

Notes: Of the second-season storylines, Read Morgan said, "I think there was an attempt at quality but television is so tough on material that it just eats it up." [258] "Day of Fear" is another interesting story from writer Clark E. Reynolds.

Episode 2.13

Second Cousin to the Czar. December 24, 1960. Written by Kay Lenard and Jess Carneol. Directed by Louis King. Produced by Michel Kraike.

Guest stars: Carl Esmond (Dimitri), George D. Wallace (Dan Farrell), Clancy Cooper (Hawkins), and Phil Tully (Charlie).

Clay is challenged to a pair of horse races during a visit to the Arizona territory by Dmitri, the self-described Duke of Tiflis. Simon bets $500 on Clay in the second race, but can't bring himself to watch.

Category: NON FONDA. Simon doesn't arrive until late in the episode, helping Clay solve the mystery.

Notes: Louis King's career in Hollywood was a long one, dating back to his first directorial effort in 1921. He was the brother of director Henry King.

Episode 2.14

Judas Town. December 31, 1960. Written by Hal Biller and Austin Kalish. Directed by Frank Arrigo. Produced by Michel Kraike.

Guest stars: Ed Nelson (Pete McCurdy), Roy Roberts (Linc McCurdy), Duane Cross (Touhy), Ed Prentiss (Mayor), Dan White (Joab), and Phil Tully (Charlie).

Wealthy businessman Linc McCurdy threatens to boycott merchants and other businesses in Silver City after Clay arrests his son and three of his men for roughing up the town and shooting a local resident. Merchants in Silver City pressure Clay to release the men, concerned that McCurdy will take his trail drive and business elsewhere.

Category: NON FONDA. Simon angers Clay by asking him to release the prisoners because it is a weak case. Simon's trying to show Silver City residents how much they actually need Clay and should trust his judgment. The plan works, as the businessman come back to Clay looking for law and order.

Notes: Frank Arrigo worked as a director, art director, production manager, assistant director, second-unit director, and producer in a Hollywood career that dated back to 1945.

Episode 2.15

Duty Bound. January 7, 1961. Repeated August 5, 1961. Written by Rod Peterson. Directed by Herschel Daugherty. Produced by Michel Kraike.

Guest stars: Ron Harper (Jay Elston), Frank Maxwell (Mel Ricker), Pat McCaffrie (Trooper), and Joe Yrigoyen (Stage Driver).

Simon, Clay, and Sgt. Tasker must escort two murder suspects through dangerous country back to Silver City. One of the suspects maintains his innocence, but the other insists the man was his accomplice. The lawmen have to fight off Indians and bandits and repair a telegraph line to do their duty and deliver the men for trial.

Category: FONDA. Simon, Clay, and Sarge share a lot of screen time in this episode, one of the highlights of the second season. The episode was shot the week of August 23, 1960, at the Oak Tree Flats location at Universal.

Notes: Ron Howard, who worked with director Daugherty on Fonda's second television series, The Smith Family, said that Daugherty was a fantastic television director in that he knew "all the tricks—staging scenes, being efficient, getting things done, he was a remarkable technician in addition to his creative talents." [259]

Episode 2.16

The Lesson. January 14, 1961. Written by Kay Lenard and Jess Carneol. Directed by Frank Arrigo. Produced by Michel Kraike.

Guest stars: Wanda Hendrix (Mary Willis), Harry Lauter (Lex Danton), Steven Darrell (Jenkins), and Kevin O'Neal (Johnny).

Silver City schoolteacher Mary Wills has been harboring a secret: her husband is an outlaw, and she's been hiding from him in Silver City. But now he's caught up to her and rides into town with his gang.

Category: NON FONDA. Simon has a long scene filling in for Mary Wills at school, teaching school children about standing up for what they believe in, quoting Benjamin Franklin and John Curran in the process.

Notes: Read Morgan said he did receive a residuals payment for his work on the series, but co-creator Norman Lear said he never received a dime, despite years of trying to find out why. [260]

Episode 2.17

Past and Present. January 21, 1961. Written by Rudy Makoul. Directed by Tay Garnett. Produced by Michel Kraike.

Guest stars: Arthur Franz (Herb Caldwell), Mary Beth Hughes (Madge Belden), Murvyn Vye (Calico Bill), Vince Williams (Sandy), and Steven Peck (Ray).

Bank clerk Herb Caldwell is ostracized by the community after he offers no resistance to an outlaw during an attempted bank robbery. Clay arrests Caldwell for not trying to stop the holdup.

Category: NON FONDA.

Notes: Most of Rudy Makoul's career credits were as a dialogue coach. He worked in that capacity for Paramount Pictures, 20th Century-Fox, and Columbia.

Episode 2.18

The Hard Decision. January 28, 1961. Repeated August 12, 1961. Written by Peggy Shaw and Lou Shaw. Directed by David Butler. Produced by Michel Kraike.

Guest stars: Marc Lawrence (Alvy Burke), George Brenlin (Jimmie Burke), Olan Soule (Dr. Stoner), John Dennis (Josh), Frank White (Clerk), and George Lynn (Hangman).

Simon brings a murder suspect into the Silver City jail for holding. The suspect's older brother kidnaps Clay and holds him in a dentist's office across the street from the jail, telling Simon he will kill the deputy unless his brother is freed. Simon refuses. The situation is reversed when Simon is held captive and Clay is free; Clay decides differently and is ready to free the prisoner when Simon manages to use the dentist's gas to knock the outlaws unconscious.

CATEGORY: FONDA. Easily the weakest of all the full FONDA episodes, "The Hard Decision" features cardboard cutout outlaws and weak acting by guest stars to boot.

Notes: Butler's directorial efforts on the series were described by authors Christopher Wicking and Tise Vahimagi as "not too pushy, not too fancy, but the stuff of a journeyman." [261]

Episode 2.19

The Dream. February 4, 1961. Written by Ellis Kadison. Directed by Tay Garnett. Produced by Michel Kraike.

Guest stars: Dick Foran (Clint Hammer), John McLiam (Ty Lawson), Carolyn Craig (Selene Hammer), and Mary Munday (Mildred Lawson).

When Clint Hammer returns to Silver City to collect his inheritance, he is angry to discover that his father didn't leave him money, but holdings. Hammer decides to collect debts owed and fire longtime loyal employees to turn the inheritance into a personal fortune.

Category: NON FONDA. Simon is seen in the middle of the first act, hanging his laundry up to dry in Clay's office. Simon appears again at the end of the episode, bringing in a gang for lock-up.

Notes: Authors Wicking and Vahimagi wrote of Tay Garnett's career: "Garnett appears to have accepted TV as naturally as he greeted all the changes that affected the business of filmmaking during his long career." [262]

Episode 2.20

The Shackled Town. February 11, 1961. Written by Clark Reynolds. Directed by Tay Garnett. Produced by Michel Kraike.

Guest stars: Carla Alberghetti (Carmelita), Robert Brubaker (Pecos Smith), Reed Hadley (Judge Denton), Eugene Iglesias (Pedro O'Brien), Ralf Harolde (Padre).

Simon forces Clay and Sgt. Tasker to go away on a vacation, but they soon regret their trip to the town of Vista Grande when they are locked in jail.

Category: NON FONDA.

Notes: More from Wicking and Vahimagi on Garnett: "Admirers of veterans like Garnett (perhaps especially Garnett, who enlivened many a dead project) do look to their small screen for his valid late work, his final statements, his parting shots, and graceful codas." They were discussing the fact that students of film, while not always looking to see how the early television work done by some major filmmakers might have affected their growth, often do, however, look at a late-in-career move to television, such as the one experienced by Tay Garnett. [263]

Episode 2.21

The Lonely Road. February 18, 1961. Repeated August 19, 1961. Written by William Leicester. Directed by Louis King. Produced by Michel Kraike.

Guest stars: Edward Binns (Shad Billings), Constance Ford (Meg Billings), Jim Davis (Trace Phelan), and Phil Tully (Charlie).

Fry fears trouble when paroled convict Shad Billings returns to Silver City looking for a fresh start. Billings' wife has been seeing gunman Trace Phelan while he has been in prison. Simon tells Phelan that if there's trouble he'll run him clear out of the territory.

Category: FONDA. Fry is seen throughout the episode; in fact, this is a rare episode in that Clay McCord does not appear at all.

Notes: There is no voice-over narration by Henry Fonda. A clip from this episode was used in the video special titled "TV's Western Heroes," a history of the television western.

Episode 2.22

The Challenger. February 25, 1961. Written by Richard Morgan. Directed by Frank Arrigo. Produced by Michel Kraike.

Guest stars: Stafford Repp (Collins), Hal Baylor (Titan), Paul Gilbert (Dillon), and Don Hietgert (Dan).

Clay and Sgt. Tasker both try boxing as a means to raise money for Clay, who needs to send money to Fran in Kansas City to help with a family emergency. Tasker demonstrates his friendship to Clay by volunteering to go into the ring.

Category: NON FONDA. Fonda appears briefly at the beginning and again at the end of the episode, talking with Clay about his salary.

Notes: For the second episode in a row, there is no voice-over narration by Henry Fonda. Richard Morgan, who wrote this episode, introduced the Sarge Tasker character in "Meet Sergeant Tasker."

Episode 2.23

The Edge of Doubt. March 4, 1961. Written by Peggy Shaw and Lou Shaw. Directed by Frank Arrigo. Produce by Michel Kraike.

Guest stars: Richard Chamberlain (Jerry Kirk), Floy Dean Smith, Bigelow C. Sayre (Will Jenner), Tommy Jackson (Mr. Potter), Floy Dean (Annie Jenner), and George Chandler (George Lake).

Recent parolee Jerry Kirk is accused of murdering his fiancée's father in Silver City. But Clay suspects a different truth and enlists Kirk in a plan to undercover the true killer and recover lost funds from a robbery years before.

Category: NON FONDA, and no Fonda narration. Simon brings Jerry Kirk in under an amnesty program before leaving to retrieve another outlaw covered by the Governor's plan.

Notes: "It was a marvelous experience," Read Morgan said of his year on the series. [264]

Episode 2.24

Two-Way Deal. March 11, 1961. Repeated August 26, 1961. Written by Roland Kibbee (story) and William E. Yagemann (teleplay). Directed by Tay Garnett. Produced by Michel Kraike.

Guest stars: Ted De Corsia (Slade Blatner), Billy Gray (Johnny Blatner), Kenneth MacDonald (Sheriff), and Nacho Galindo (Sancho).

Slade Blatner wants the $1800 reward promised for bringing in an outlaw to marshal Fry. The outlaw in this case is his own son.

Category: FONDA.

Notes: One last story from series co-creator Roland Kibbee. How the series might have been different had he and co-creator Norman Lear stayed with it is something, of course, that will never be known.

Episode 2.25

The Means and the End. March 18, 1961. Repeated September 2, 1961. Written by Clark Reynolds. Directed by Tay Garnett. Produced by Michel Kraike.

Guest stars: DeForest Kelley (Farley Styles), Phyllis Love (Josie Styles), Justice Watson (Judge), Robert E. Griffin (Wiley), Richard Warren (Lon Spivak), and Don Heitgert (Clerk).

Simon arrests outlaw Josie Styles and locks her up in the Silver City jail. Publicly, Simon says she will hang for her crimes. Privately, he hopes that by locking her up and threatening to hang her, he will lure in Josie's husband, Farley Styles, another wanted outlaw.

Category: FONDA. Very enjoyable episode watching two Hollywood veterans, Fonda and DeForest Kelley, engage in a battle of wits, before the climatic gun battle.

Notes: An admirable attempt on the part of the producers and writer Clark Reynolds to try something a little different with a story—a marshal threatening to hang a woman was not a common sight among television westerns of the late 1950s and early 1960s.

Episode 2.26

The Example. March 25, 1961. Written by Ralph Goodman. Directed by Otto Lang. Produced by Michel Kraike.

Guest stars: Denver Pyle (Frank Barton), Jack Chaplain (Jeb Barton), Rick Sorensen (Kitt), Reedy Talton (Whitney), Phil Tully (Charlie), and Robert C. Ross (Gabe).

Clay is worried about young Jeb Barton, a teenager who is showing all the signs of wanting to emulate his father, outlaw Frank Barton. Clay hatches a scheme to go below the border to find the elder Barton in hopes of convincing him to return to Silver City to have a talk with the boy, with the understanding that he won't be arrested. Simon tells Clay that officially he can't sanction the plan, but that unofficially he wishes he had thought of it.

Category: NON FONDA. Simon appears at the beginning of the episode when Clay discusses his plan, and then again at the end to see what happened. There is no voice-over narration by Fonda.

Notes: Director Otto Lang said his work on the series gave him "the rare opportunity to direct Henry Fonda in a television appearance." [265]

Episode 2.27

Cherchez La Femme. April 1, 1961. Written by Stuart Jerome. Directed by David Butler. Produced by Michel Kraike.

Guest stars: Lisa Montell (Rosaria Martinez), Edward C. Platt (Noah Harper), Phil Tully (Charlie).

Clay searches for the woman who can clear Sgt. Tasker of a murder charge. Tasker was protecting the woman from a man when he accidentally killed him. The woman, the only witness to the accident, has disappeared.

Category: NON FONDA.

Notes: Of his work as a director in television, David Butler said, "The main thing in TV was that you had to make the pictures on time. You couldn't run over because they had a set price for each picture. If you ran over a day or more, that added to the cost, and that was the end of you." [266]

Episode 2.28

Tension Point. April 8, 1961. Repeated September 9, 1961. Written by Clark Reynolds. Directed by Tay Garnett. Produced by Michel Kraike.

Guest stars: Jerome Thor (Ben Meadows), John Marley (Zeb Baker), Virginia Christine (Molly Baker), William Stevens (Whip), Donald Losby (Mark Baker), and Bern Hoffman (Club).

A posse led by Simon kills an outlaw who turns out to be the son of people Simon has known for twenty years. While Clay and Sgt. Tasker track the rest of the outlaw's gang, Simon visits the dead man's family. The remaining gang members double back, however, and hold Simon and the family hostage. Simon conceals his identity to prevent harm to the family.

Category: FONDA. Simon is trapped in a claustrophobic battle of wits with the outlaw gang in the family's home.

Notes: Clark Reynolds, a major writer during the second season, is sometimes confused with an actor with a similar name. The actor appeared in Westerns made in Germany.

Episode 2.29

Brother in Arms. April 15, 1961. Written by Edward J. Lakso. Directed by David Butler. Produced by Michel Kraike.

Guest stars: Denny Miller (Bill Jason), Lon Chaney, Jr. (Tom Arnold), and Bill Hale (Garth Cabot).

A boyhood friend of Clay's, Bill Jason, returns to Silver City. He was taught how to shoot by Clay's father, Luke McCord, but has returned with a killer's reputation. When Jason hesitates to draw on Tom Arnold, Clay convinces Jason that his gun fighting days are over.

Category: NON FONDA. Simon discusses a mail burglary ring with Clay at the beginning of the episode, and questions Jason after a shooting in the saloon.

Notes: Of Lon Chaney, Jr., Read Morgan said, "Boy, he was a powerful guy. I could understand how he could do the Wolf Man. There was a scene in the show where I had to grab him and hold him and it was all I could do to do that." [267]

Episode 2.30
The Return of Widow Brown. April 22, 1961. Written by Norman Jacob. Directed by Otto Lang. Produced by Michel Kraike.

Guest stars: Norma Crane (Amelia Brown), Richard Shannon (Chuck Beloyne), Jeff DeBenning (Henry Colton), Tom Greenway (Warden Binns), and Dennis Holmes (Tommy Brown).

Amelia Brown and her young son return to Silver City, years after her outlaw husband was killed before he could tell anyone where he had hidden stolen money. Amelia says she has no idea where the money is, and Clay believes her, but he must find the money to help the family move on with their lives.

Category: NON FONDA. Simon discusses the difficulties being faced by Amelia Brown with Clay, but the episode, as ever, belongs to Allen Case.

Notes: This is one of the series episodes—another is "The Hard Decision"—that passed out of copyright, into public domain, and onto home video rental compilations, before being reclaimed under copyright laws.

Episode 2.31

Spoken in Silence. April 29, 1961. Repeated September 16, 1961. Written by Kay Lenard and Jess Carneol. Directed by Tay Garnett. Produced by Michel Kraike.

Guest stars: Robert Burton (Mike Rogers), Frances Helm (Laura), Sydney Pollack (Chuck Johnson), and Hal K. Dawson (Sam).

Needing money for his deaf and mute daughter's operation, Mike Rogers agrees to help an outlaw elude Simon Fry.

Category: FONDA.

Notes: This episode was officially the last episode to be broadcast during the series' run on NBC- TV, a repeat in September.

Episode 2.32

An Enemy of the Town. May 6, 1961. Written by Jerry Sackheim and Curtis Kenyon. Directed by Frank Arrigo. Produced by Michel Kraike.

Guest stars: Whit Bissell (Will Culp), Ray Kellogg (Quent Hall), Stephen Roberts (Adam Crockett), and Addison Richards (Doc Landy).

Newspaper editor Will Culp suspects the run-off from a new tannery in Silver City is polluting the local water supply. But any investigation he might launch is cut short when the owner of the tannery threatens to expose the fact that Culp fled the scene of a killing, years before. Clay, however, closes the tannery down when water tests prove the run-off has made some local citizen sick and killed others. Local businessmen, who doubt the reliability of the tests, demand that Clay allow the tannery to reopen.

Category: NON FONDA, and there is no voice-over narration from Fonda. Simon fires on the townspeople threatening to hang the tannery owner once the truth is known.

Notes: Shades of Henrik Ibsen and kudos once again to the producers for at least trying something different—a story including personal redemption on the part of the newspaperman, and the scientific testing of the local water supply.

Episode 2.33

The Legend of Dixie. May 20, 1961. Written by Robert Sabaroff. Directed by Frank Arrigo. Produced by Michel Kraike.

Guest stars: Stanley Adams (Dixie Miller), Gregory Walcott (Gar Logan), Harry Fleer (Mace), and King Calder (Hoak).

Vagrant Dixie Miller basks in his new-found fame when local citizens give him credit for killing two fugitives after he is found standing over the bodies of the two outlaws with a gun in his hand.

Category: NON FONDA.

Notes: Read Morgan and Allen Case later worked together again in an episode of *Police Woman* in 1976 titled "Task Force." The two-part episode was meant as a series pilot, but the spin-off didn't sell.

Episode 2.34

The Deathly Quiet. May 27, 1961. Written by Paul Franklin. Directed by Otto Lang. Produced by Michel Kraike.

Guest stars: Johnny Cash (Bo Braddock), Robert Foulk (Colonel Belknap), Michael Garrett (Con Hawkins), Craig Duncan (Ed Walsh), and Chubby Johnson (Stonewall Brown).

Simon, Clay, and Sgt. Tasker do battle with a pair of Army deserters who have stolen a pair of Gatling guns from a secret convoy, made up to look like a grub wagon, and are shooting up the territory.

Category: NON FONDA. Simon makes plans with Clay and Sarge, after prying the secret information out of Sarge, but isn't seen again until the end of the episode.

Notes: Country music legend Johnny Cash does not sing in this episode.

Episode 2.35

Brand of Honesty. June 10, 1961. Written by Herbert Purdom. Directed by Tay Garnett. Produced by Michel Kraike.

Guest stars: Elisha Cook, Jr. (Miller), George Dolenz (Ramon

Ortega), Edward McKinley (John Gardner), Norman Willis (Brandon Clark), and Robert Osterloh (Nathans).

In this humorous episode from Herb Purdom, two former criminals have to take steps to clear themselves when the residents of Silver City suspect them of being behind a series of recent robberies. The two round-up the real culprits, forcing Simon to fudge the report to the Commissioner so he and his deputy don't look foolish.

Category: NON FONDA, and there is no voice-over narration from Fonda. Allen Case narrates. Simon has a meeting in Clay's office with Ramon Ortega.

Notes: Tay Garnett said that one of the things that made *The Deputy* set such a happy one for him was the work of "Curly Linden, the fastest cameraman on the lot." [268]

Episode 2.36

Lorinda Belle. June 24, 1961. Written by Rik Vollaerts (story, teleplay) and Michel Kraike (teleplay). Directed by Sherry Shourds. Produced by Michel Kraike.

Guest stars: Claude Akins (Jason Getty), Frank Overton (Bill Corman), Andy Albin (Zack Martinson), and Addison Richards (Doc Landy).

Local mine owner Jason Getty has two days to live because of a slow-acting poison someone gave him. He's determined to find out who has murdered him. Clay discovers that Getty was poisoned by Bill Corman, who has hated Getty ever since a woman he loved left him for Getty. Lorinda Belle committed suicide after Getty abandoned her.

Category: NON FONDA, and there is no voice-over narration by Henry Fonda. Simon and Clay talk over a campfire and devise a plan to find the killer.

Notes: Director Sherry Shrouds worked mostly as an assistant director, and was nominated for an Academy Award in that capacity in 1936.

Episode 2.37

Lawman's Conscience. July 1, 1961.Written by Saul Schwartz (story) and Michel Kraike (teleplay). Directed by Frederick Stephani. Produced by Michel Kraike.

Guest stars: Russell Johnson (Albie Beckett), Tracey Roberts (Mary Hayden), Jason Robards, Sr. (Rufus Hayden), Jerry LaZarre (Zack Tanby), and Roy Wright (Phil Briggs).

When rancher Rufus Hayden gives a deathbed confession clearing Albee Beckett of a murder charge, Beckett is freed from the prison where he'd been serving a life term. However, Beckett returns to Silver City seeking vengeance against the people who convicted him.

Category: NON FONDA.

Notes: This was the last original episode seen on NBC. "I wish it could have gone on, but I understand why it didn't," Read Morgan said. "On the other hand, I was always happy being a freelance actor." [269]

Endnotes

1   "Singing in the Rain," *Newsweek,* page 83.

2   Fonda, "Hank Fonda Talks about New Series," page 7G

3   *Newsweek,* page 83.

4   McManus, page 6

5   *Newsweek,* page 83

6   Ibid, page 83.

7   Goldstein, page 37

8   Kleiner, TV Section, page 1

9   Smith, 9/11/59, pageA8

10   Buscombe, page 404

11   Smith, 11/16/70, page G21

12   Salmaggi, page 21

13   Parkinson, 1975.

14   Goldstein, page 37.

15   Buscombe, page 342

16   Lear, personal interview

17   Bogdanovich, "Who the Hell's in It?" page 302.

18   Morgan, personal interview

19   Bogdanovich, "Who the Devil Made It," page 805

20   Bogdanovich, "Who the Hell's in it?" page 302.

21   Goldin, RadioGoldIndex

22   Billips, page 59

23   Goldstein, page 37

24   TV Guide, page 14

25   McManus, August 16, 1959

26   "The Marshal's on the Level," TV Guide, page 14

27   TV- Radio Life, August 27, 1954, page 40

28   Smith, August 2, 1959

29   Grobel, page 132.

30   McManus, August 16, 1959

31   Morgan, personal interview

32   Optowsky, page 107

33   "Singing in the Rain," *Newsweek,* page 83

34   McManus, August 16, 1959

35   "The Marshal's on the Level," TV Guide, page 14

36   Ibid

37   "Henry Frys About Simon," April 10, 1960, page 12

38   "Henry Frys About Simon," April 10, 1960, page 12

39   The Fonda segment of this script is part of the Robert Sincalir Teleplays Collection at USC- Santa Barbara.

40   "The Marshal's on the Level," TV Guide, page 14

41   "Fonda Fans Nettled by His No- Show," December 13, 1959

42   Ibid

43   "The Marshal's on the Level," *TV Guide,* page 14

44   Morgan, personal interview

45   Ibid

46   "Hank Fonda Talks About New Series," September 6, 1959

47   Korman, March 12, 1960

48   Morgan, personal interview

49   Garnett, page 311

50   "Fonda Fans Nettled by His No- Show," December 13, 1959

51   Smith, August 2, 1959

52   McManus, August 16, 1959

53   *Variety,* September 16, 1959

54   Denton, October 25, 1959

55   McManus, August 16, 1959

56   Shay, page 70

57   *St. Petersburg Times,* February 27, 1960

58   *The Milwaukee Sentinel,* March 28, 1960

59   *TV Guide,* June 18, 1960, page 23

60   Yoggy, page 168

61   "The Means and the End" written by Clarke Reynolds.

62   "The Last Gunfight," written by Richard Carr (story) and
     Charles B. Smith (teleplay)

63   Topping, page 299

64   Korman, June 4, 1960

65   Fonda, August 15, 1961

66   Morgan, personal interview

67   Ibid

68   Smith, November 16, 1970

69   Sherman, September 4, 1959, page B 5

70   Fonda, August 15, 1961

71   Morgan, personal interview

72   Smith, August 2, 1959

73   For an excellent treatment on the subject of film stars working
     in 1950s series television, see Christine Becker's book *It's the
     Pictures That Got Small,* Wesleyan University Press, 2008

74   Teichman, page 265

75   Writer's Presentation, page 17

76   "Back to Glory," written by Charles B. Smith, broadcast September 26, 1959

77   Kirkley, page 133

78   Writer's Presentation, page 17

79   See chapter 5 for more on "Hang the Law."

80   Ibid, page 19

81   Salmaggi, page 21

82   "The Silent Gun," written by Rik Vollaerts

83   Writer's Presentation, page 19

84   Garver, e- mail, December 14, 2009

85   Morgan, personal interview

86   "Now He's a Singing Star," page 9

87   Thompson, page 1

88   The pilot was *Ivy League,* executive- produced by Alan Ladd. It aired on *Schlitz Playhouse of Stars* on March 13, 1959.

89   "Musical Comedy Singer Goes West," *TV Guide,* page 23

90   "Musical Comedy Singer Goes West," *TV Guide,* page 23

91   Ibid, page 23

92   Morgan, personal interview

93   Ibid

94   Thompson, page 11

95   "Musical Comedy Singer Goes West," *TV Guide,* page 23

96   Ibid

97   Barnes, page H 2

98   Pearson, March 23, 1960, page B 11.

99   Korman, "The Luckiest Deputy," page C 3

100 Pearson, "Case Predicts Bigger Future for Self," page B 2

101 Gould, page 59

102 Korman, "The Luckiest Deputy," page C 3

103 Pearson, "Case Predicts Bigger Future for Self," page B 2

104 Garver, e- mail, December 14, 2009

105 Ibid

106 Pearson, "Case Predicts Bigger Future for Self," page B 2

107 "Now He's a Singing Star," TV- Radio Dial, page 9

108 Berlinger, e- mail, December 24, 2009

109 Allen Case might have been surprised to discover that *The Deputy* was one of the series cited in 1961 by then-outgoing NBC vice-president in charge of TV programs David Levy as containing a high level of violence (MacDonald, "Who Shot the Sheriff?" page 92).

110 Pearson, "Case Predicts Bigger Future for Self," page B 2

111 "The Silent Gun," broadcast January 23, 1960, written by Rik Vollaerts

112 Writers' Presentation, page 20

113 Ibid, page 21

114 Ibid, page 21

115 "The Border Between," broadcast March 12, 1960, written by Hal Biller and Austin Kalish

116 Jenkins, February 6, 1960, page 3

117 Berlinger, e- mail, December 24, 2009

118 Kilgallen, page 18

119 Barnes, *The Hollywood Reporter,* February 4, 2010

120 Writers' Presentation, page 24

121 "Focus of Doom" written by Michel Kraike and Sidney Michaels

122 Writers' Presentation, page 24

123 Morgan, personal interview

124 Hannsberry, page 249

125 Writers' Presentation, page 25

126 "Badge for a Day," written by Roland Kibbee and Norman Lear.

127 Morgan, personal interview

128 Ibid

129 Morgan, personal interview

130 Finnegan, page 14

131 Ibid

132 Morgan, personal interview

133 Morgan, personal interview

134 Lear, personal interview

135 Ibid

136 "Writer Becomes Producer," July 17, 1972

137 Lear, Archive of American Television interview

138 See the Center's web site at www.learcenter.org

139 Lear, personal interview

140 Perry, page xii

141 McCarty, page x.

142 Ibid, page xvi

143 Warren, page 14

144 Morgan, personal interview

145 Butler, page 272

146 *The Marshall Swings*, album notes

147 Field, page 272

148 Holder, page 10

149 Topping, page 291

150 Cawelti, page 189

151 "The Crockett Craze," Disney Enterprises, 2001

152 Newcomb, "TV: The Most Popular Art." page 248.

153 Barson, page 67

154 *Badge for a Day*, written by Roland Kibbee and Norman Lear, September 12, 1959.

155 Fonda, *The Hartford Courant*, page 7G

156 *Badge for a Day*, By Roland Kibbee and Norman Lear, 1959.

157 Ibid

158 Smith, "Formulas Needn't Stifle originality," page A10

159 Kerns, Sec. I, page 6

160 *Broadcasting*, Vol. 57, number 13.

161 *Variety*, September 16, 1959

162 Wicking, page 66.

163 Those sources include *All Movie Guide, Cult Movies,* and *The BFI Companion to the Western*.

164 Writer's Presentation, page 6

165 *The Tin Star*, written by Dudley Nichols, Paramount Pictures, 1957.

166 Buscombe, page 218.

167 "The Two Faces of Bob Claxton," By Charles O'Neal, NBC-TV, February 27, 1960

168 Lear, personal interview

169 Ibid

170 Writer's Presentation, page 27

171 "Badge for a Day," written by Roland Kibbee and Norman Lear

172 Lear, personal interview

173 "Badge for a Day," Kibbee and Lear

174 Writer's Presentation, page 2

175 Kirkley, page 169

176 "The Lonely Road," written by William F. Leicester

177 Writer's Presentation, page 6

178 Ibid, page 6

179 "Man of Peace," By Roland Kibbee (story) and Herbert Purdom (teleplay).

180 Writer's Presentation, pages 9- 10

181 Ibid, page 13

182 Writer's Presentation, page 11

183 Kirkley, page 178

184 Gruber, pages 5- 7

185 Writer's Presentation, page 15

186 Ibid, page 15- 16

187 Writer's Presentation, page 16

188 *Broadcasting,* vol. 57, # 14, page 45

189 Ibid, page 35

190 *Broadcasting,* vol. 57, # 14, page 36

191 Barnouw, page 128

192 Macdonald, "*One Nation,*" page 172.

193 *Variety,* September 16, 1959

194 "Shadow of the Noose," written by Roland Kibbee, page 9.

195 Fonda, "My Life," page 26.

196 Kibbee, "Shadow of the Noose," page 2

197 Ibid, page 3

198 Ibid, page 3

199 Kibbee, "Shadow of the Noose," page 6

200 Ibid, page 11

201 Kibbee, "Shadow of the Noose," page 34.

202 Kennedy, page 103.

203 Sinclair, Cast Sheet

204 Sinclair, Shooting Schedule

205 Ibid

206 Sinclair, Shooting Schedule

207 Ibid

208 Sinclair, Shooting Schedule

209 Sinclair, Shooting Schedule

210 Kibbee, "Shadow of the Noose," page 2.

211 "Hang the Law," written by Herbert Purdom, page 10.

212 "Hang the Law," page 16

213 "Hang the Law," page 24.

214 "Hang the Law," page 6

215 "Hang the Law," shooting schedule, page 2

216 Scott, page 12

217 Scott, page 12

218 Lowry, TV section, page 5

219 Scott, page 12

220 Howard, Archives of American Television interview

221 Ibid

222 Stephens, page 68

223 McCaffrey, page 80

224 Swain, page 6 B

225 Shay, page 70

226 Purser, page 45

227 Kiernan, page 106

228 Ibid

229 Morgan, personal interview

230 *Broadcasting,* September 28, 1959, page 62

231 Ibid

232 Ibid

233 See, for example, "The Miraculous Journey of Tadpole Chan" from *The Barbara Stanwyck Show,* broadcast November 14, 1960.

234 "Henry Frys About Simon," April 10, 1960, page 12

235 Carey, page 152

236 Garnett, page 311

237 Dube, "Dial Turns," page 12

238 Whitbeck, page G 10.

239 Salmaggi, page 21

240 Lubin, page 91

241 Morgan, personal interview

242 Smith, September 15, 1959, page A 10

243 Gibson, page 25.

244 Edelman, page 238

245 Whitbeck, page G 10

246 Dube, "Dial Turns," page 12

247 Whitbeck, page G 10

248 Jenkins, February 6, 1960, page 3

249 Royal, page 9

250 United States Copyright Office, web site

251 Script by Ellis Kadison

252 Hopper, May 13, 1962, page M 5

253 Dixon, page 115

254 Morgan, personal interview

255 Munn, page 304

256 Munn, page 304

257 Wicking, page 129

258 Morgan, personal interview

259 Howard, Archive of American Television interview

260 Lear, Morgan, personal interviews

261 Wicking, page 121

262 Wicking, page 125

263 Wicking, page 125

264 Morgan, personal interview

265 Lang, page 388

266 Butler, page 267

267 Morgan, personal interview

268 Garnett, page 311

269 Morgan, personal interview

Bibliography

ARTICLES

Adams, Val. "New NBC Western Slated." *The New York Times*. June 2, 1959.

Adams, Val. "Fonda to Expand Role in 'Deputy.'" *The New York Times*. March 21, 1960.

"Allen Case, TV Star in 'The Deputy'" *The Chicago Tribune*. August 25, 1986.

Anderson, Robert. "TV Gets 4 Big Doses of Action." *The Chicago Tribune*. September 15, 1959.

Barnes, Aleene. "Deputy Badge Hides a Case for Singing." *The Los Angeles Times*. March 6, 1960.

Barnes, Mike. "Actress Betty Lou Keim Dies." *The Hollywood Reporter*. February 4, 2010.

Beck, Marilyn. "Fonda Keeps Fit for New TV Series." *The Hartford Courant*. December 21, 1970.

Byrne, Julie. "Thespians Getting into the Fashion Act." *The Los Angeles Times*. July 16, 1969.

Coggins, Amos. "Actor by Accident." *The Milwaukee Sentinel*, 'The American Weekly.' February 19, 1961.

Crosby, John. "He's Surprised to Find This One on the TV Cable." *The Washington Post*. January 21, 1955.

Crosby, John. "Fall Season Arrives; Three New Entries." *The Hartford Courant*. September 16, 1959.

Danzig, Fred. "Television Review." *The Sarasota Journal*. September 27, 1960.

Denton, Charles. "TV From Hollywood." *The Hartford Courant*. October 25, 1959.

Dube, Bernard. "Dial Turns." *The Montreal Gazette*. September 10, 1959.

"Ex- Director Found Slain." *The Los Angeles Times*. January 5, 1970.

Finnegan, Joe. "Semi Invalids Popular in TV Programs." *The Lodi News Sentinel*. November 21, 1960.

Folkhart, Burt A. "Howard Roberts; Jazz Guitarist Played on 2,000 Recordings." *The Los Angeles Times*. July 3, 1992.

Fonda, Henry. "Hank Fonda Talks About New Series." *The Hartford Courant*. September 6, 1959.

"Fonda Fans Nettled By His No Show." *The Hartford Courant*. December 13, 1959.

"Fonda's Cowboy Image Has Him Stumped." *The Chicago Tribune*. September 18, 1960.

Fonda, Henry. "The Deputy Proves Non- Violent Westerns Can Sustain Interest." *St. Petersburg Times*. August 15, 1961.

Godbout, Oscar. "Terhune Stories will be TV Series." *The New York Times*. March 13, 1957.

Gould, Jack. "TV: On Opening a Season. NBC Offers Saturday Night Series Starring Henry Fonda in Western." *The New York Times*. September 14, 1959.

Grobel, Lawrence. "The Playboy Interview: Henry Fonda." *Playboy*. December, 1980.

Gruber, Frank. "Seven Ways to Plot a Western." *TV Guide*. August 30, 1958.

"Henry Fonda Speaks His Mind." *TV- Radio Life*, August 27, 1954.

"Henry Frys about Simon." *Ocala Star- Banner, All Florida TV Week Magazine*, April 10, 1960.

Hopper, Hedda. "Hollywood." *The Hartford Courant*. April 6, 1960.

Hopper, Hedda. "Vince Edwards: Big Operator Now." *The Los Angeles Times*. May 13, 1962.

Jenkins, Dan. "A New Generation of Giants." *TV Guide*. November 17, 1959.

Jenkins, Dan. "TV Teletype—Hollywood." *TV Guide.* February 6, 1960.

Kerns, Janet. "Networks Hurl 5 New Shows Into TV Ring." *The Milwaukee Sentinel.* September 16, 1959.

Kilgallen, Dorothy. "Voice of Broadway." *The Schenectaday Gazette.* June 9, 1961.

Kleiner, Dick. "Henry Fonda Turns to TV." *The Fort Scott Tribune,* August 14, 1970.

Korman, Seymour. "The Bigger They Come, the Harder They Fall for TV." *The Chicago Tribune.* March 12, 1960.

Korman, Seymour. "The Luckiest Deputy." *Chicago Daily Tribune.* June 4, 1960.

Leonard, Vince. "TV Movies of Paramount Importance." *The Pittsburgh Press.* August 28, 1968.

Lowry, Cynthia. "Henry Fonda Happy Star of TV Series." *The Schenectady Gazette.* February 27, 1971.

"The Marshal's on the Level." *TV Guide.* January 23, 1960.

McManus, Margaret. "Marshal Simon: Henry Fonda Will Have Own TV Series." *The Miami News.* August 16, 1959.

Mercer, Charles. "Fonda Says Yes at Last to TV Western Series." *The Hartford Courant,* August 9, 1959.

"Musical- Comedy Singer Goes West." *TV Guide.* June 18, 1960.

"The Ninety Day Mistress." *St. Petersburg Times.* September 2, 1973.

"Now He's a Singing Star." *St. Petersburg Times.* May 6, 1962.

Pearson, Howard. "Allen Case Predicts Bigger Future for Self." *The Deseret News and Telegram.* January 9, 1960.

Pearson, Howard. "Mysteries, Adventures to Dominate New TV Fare." *The Deseret News and Telegram.* March 23, 1960.

"Perfection Pays Big Dividends." *Chicago Daily Tribune.* October 30, 1960.

Purser, Philip. "Putting it on Film." *Sight and Sound,* by the British Film Institute, vol. 29- 32, 1959.

"Read Morgan's Fitness Program." *TV Guide.* January 28, 1961.

"Ready for Action." *The Hartford Courant.* September 6, 1959.

"Roland Kibbee, 70; Emmy- Winning Writer." *The Los Angeles Times.* August 7, 1984.

Royal, Don. "Meet Allen Case." *The Southeast Missourian.* February 26, 1960.

Salmaggi, Bob. "Henry Fonda Says 'The Deputy' Not Just another Hosting Deal." *The Tuscaloosa News.* September 6, 1959.

Scott, Vernon. "In Hollywood." *The Bryan Times.* January 13, 1971.

Sherman, Gene. "It's so Continental on S'Monica Blvd." *The Los Angeles Times.* September 4, 1959.

"Singing in the Rain." *Newsweek.* August 16, 1959.

Smith, Cecil. "Fonda Saddles Up for Bright Series." *The Los Angeles Times.* August 2, 1959.

Smith, Cecil. "Man Barricades! Oscar's Returning." *The Los Angeles Times.* September 11, 1959.

Smith, Cecil. "Formulas Needn't Stifle Originality." *The Los Angeles Times.* September 15, 1959.

Smith, Cecil. "Why Hank Fonda Returned to TV." *The Los Angeles Times.* November 16, 1970.

"Special Report: A Hard Look at the Fall Lineup." *Broadcasting,* September 28, 1959, vol. 57, #13.

Stansfield, Robert E. "Seven New Entries Mark Opening of Fall Season." *The Hartford Courant.* September 6, 1959.

Swain, Harrison. "Television in a Rut, says Rod Serling." *St. Petersburg Independent.* November 4, 1966.

"Sweaters Do More Than Keep You Warm." *TV Guide.* January 16, 1960.

Thackrey Jr., Ted. "Henry Fonda Dies Peacefully at 77, Wife at his Side." *The Los Angeles Times.* August 12, 1982.

Thompson, Ruth. "Jesse James' Star Alternates Musicals, Westerns." *The Gettysburg Times.* December 4, 1965.

Topping, M.C., Jr. "The Cultural Orientation of Certain Western Characters on Television." *Journal of Broadcasting.* Fall 1965, Vol. IX, no. 4, pgs. 291- 304.

"The Two Faces of Bob Claxton." *The St. Petersburg Times.* February 27, 1960.

"TV Notes." *The Hartford Courant.* April 30, 1961.

"Unusual Horse Epic in Making." *The Los Angeles Times.* September 6, 1959.

"Wallace Ford is Dead at 68." *The New York Times.* June 12, 1966.

"Wilson of CBS Gets New Project." *The New York Times.* March 20, 1956.

Witbeck, Charles. "Deputy is Western 'Father Knows Best.'" *The Modesto Bee.* January 24, 1960.

Wolters, Larry. "You Ain't Seen Nuthin' Yet! More Westerns are Due on TV." *Chicago Daily Tribune.* August 9, 1959.

Wolters, Larry. "TV Ticker." *Chicago Tribune.* April 1, 1961.

Wolters, Larry. "TV's Jerking Some Tear Jerkers, Too." *Chicago Tribune.* May 15, 1961.

"Writer Becomes Producer, Almost in Self- Defense." *The Rock Hill Herald.* July 17, 1972.

"The X Game." *The Milwaukee Sentinel.* March 28, 1960.

BOOKS

Anderson, Christopher. "Hollywood TV: The Studio System in the Fifties." Austin, Texas: University of Texas Press, 1994.

Barnouw, Eric. "The Image Empire." New York, New York: Oxford University Press, 1970.

Becker, Christine. "It's the Pictures That Got Small—Hollywood Film Stars on 1950s Television." Middletown, Connecticut: Wesleyan University Press, 2008.

Billips, Connie, and Arthur Pierce. "Lux Presents Hollywood." Jefferson, North Carolina: McFarland Publishers, Inc., 1995.

Bogdanovich, Peter. "Who the Devil Made It." New York, New York: Alfred A. Knopf, 1997.

Bogdanovich, Peter. "Who the Hell's In It." New York, New York: Alfred A. Knopf, 2004.

Buscombe, Edward. "The BFI Companion to the Western." New York, New York: Atheneum, 1988.

Butler, David, interviewed by Irene Kahn Atkins. "David Butler." Metuchen, New Jersey & London: The Directors Guild of America and the Scarecrow Press, Inc., 1993.

Carey, Jr., Harry. "Company of Heroes." Metuchen, New Jersey & London: The Scarecrow Press, 1994.

Cawelti, John G. "The Six Gun Mystique Sequel." Bowling Green, Ohio: Bowling Green State University Popular Press, 1999.

Dixon, Wheeler W. "The Films of Reginald Le Borg." Metuchen, NJ: The Scarecrow Press, 1992.

Dunning, John. "On the Air: the Encyclopedia of Old- Time Radio." New York, New York: Oxford University Press, 1998.

Edelman, Rob, with Audrey Kupferberg. "Meet the Mertzes—The Life Stories of *I Love Lucy's* Other Couple." Los Angeles, Ca: Renaissance Books, 1999.

Field, Kim. "Harmonicas, Harps, and Heavy Breathers: The Evolution of the People's Instrument." New York, New York: Cooper Square Press, 2000.

Fireman, Judy. "TV Book." New York, New York: Workman Publishing Company, 1977.

Fonda, Henry, with Howard Teichmann. "My Life." New York, New York: New American Library, 1981.

Fraser, George MacDonald. "The Hollywood History of the World." New York, New York: Fawcett Columbine, 1988.

Garnett, Tay, with Fredda Dudley Balling. "Light Your Torches and Pull Up Your Tights." New Rochelle, New York: Arlington House, 1973.

Gibson, William. "The Seesaw Log." New York, New York: Alfred A. Knopf, 1959.

Goldstein, Norman. "Henry Fonda." New York, New York: Holt, Rinehart, and Winston, 1982.

Hannsberry, Karen Burroughs. "Bad Boys. The Actors of Film Noir." Jefferson, North Carolina: McFarland Publishers, Inc., 2003.

Hawes, William. "Live Television Drama, 1946- 1951." Jefferson, North Carolina: McFarland Publishers, Inc., 2001.

Holder, Mitch. "Mel Bay Presents the Jazz Guitar Stylings of Howard Roberts." Pacific, Missouri: Mel Bay Publications, Inc, 2006.

Inman, David. "The TV Encyclopedia." New York, New York: Perigee Books, 1991.

Katz, Ephraim. "The Film Encyclopedia." New York, New York: Harper Collins, 1998.

Kennedy, Burt. "Hollywood Trail Boss." New York, New York: Boulevard Books, 1997.

Kiernan, Thomas. "Jane: An Intimate Biography of Jane Fonda." New York, New York: G.P. Putnam's Sons, 1973.

Kirkley Jr., Donald H. "A Descriptive Study of the Network Television Western During the Seasons 1955- 56- 1962- 63." New York, New York: Arno Press, 1979.

Lang, Otto. "A Bird of Passage: The Story of My Life." Helena, MT: Skyhouse Publishers, 1994.

Lentz, Harris M. "Television Westerns Episode Guide: All United States Series 1949- 1996." Jefferson, North Carolina: McFarland Publishers, Inc, 1997.

Lubin, Arthur, interviewed by James Desmarais. "Arthur Lubin." A Directors Guild of America Oral History, 1976- 1977.

Maltin, Leonard. "Leonard Maltin's Movie Encyclopedia." New York, New York: Penguin Books, 1994.

MacDonald, J. Fred. "One Nation Under Television." New York, New York: Pantheon Books, 1990.

MacDonald, J. Fred. "Who Shot the Sheriff? The Rise and Fall of the Television Western." New York, New York: Praeger, 1987.

McCaffrey, Donald W. "Bound and Gagged in Hollywood: Edmund L. Hartmann, Screenwriter and Producer." Lanham, MD: The Scarecrow Press, 2006.

McCarty, John, and Brian Kelleher. "Alfred Hitchcock Presents." New York, New York, St. Martin's Press, 1984.

Munn, Michael. "John Wayne" The Man Behind the Myth." London, England: Robson Books, 2003.

Navasky, Victor S. "Naming Names." New York, New York: Hill and Wang, 2003.

Newcomb, Horace. "TV: The Most Popular Art." Garden City, New York: The Anchor Press, 1974.

Opotowsky, Stan. "TV, The Big Picture." New York, New York: Dutton, 1961.

Peary, Danny. "Cult Movies." New York, New York: Delacorte Press, 1961.

Perry, Jeb H. "Universal Television: The Studio and its Programs, 1950- 1980." Metuchen, New Jersey: Scarecrow Press, 1983.

Shay, Don. "Conversations, Volume I." Albuquerque, New Mexico: Kaleidoscope Press, 1969.

Shulman, Arthur, and Roger Youman. "The Golden Age of Television." New York, New York: Bonanza Books, 1979.

Stephens, John G. "From My Three Sons to Major Dad: My Life as TV Producer." Lanham, Maryland: The Scarecrow Press, 2005.

Sweeney, Kevin. "Henry Fonda: A Bio- Bibliography." New York, New York: Greenwood Press. 1992.

Thomas, Tony. "The Complete Films of Henry Fonda." Secaucus, New Jersey: Citadel Press, 1983.

Warren, Alan. "This is a Thriller." Jefferson, North Carolina: McFarland Publishers, Inc., 2004.

West, Richard. "Television Westerns." Jefferson, North Carolina: McFarland Publishers, Inc., 1987.

Wicking, Christopher, with Tise Vahimagi. "The American Vein: Directors and Directions in American Television." New York, New York: E.P. Dutton, 1979.

Yoggy, Gary A. "Riding the Video Range, the Rise and Fall of the Western on Television." Jefferson, North Carolina: McFarland Publishers, Inc., 1995.

WEBSITES

The Archive of American Television, Norman Lear interview, conducted by Morrie Gelman, dated February 26, 1998. www.emmystvlegends.org

The Archive of American Television, Ron Howard interview, conducted by Gary Rutkowski, dated October 18, 2006. www.emmytvlegends.org

BFI Film and TV Database, www.bfi.org.uk/filmtvinfo/ftvdb

The Classic TV Archive, http://ctva.biz/index.htm

The Internet Broadway Database, www.ibdb.com

The Internet Movie Database, www.imdb.com

Radio Gold Index, www.radiogoldindex.com

UCLA Film and TV Archive, http://catalogcin.library.ucla.edu

The United States Copyright Office, http://cocatalog.loc.gov

Worldcat, www.worldcat.org

OTHER SOURCES

Berlinger, Warren. E-mail correspondence. December 24, 2009.

Case, Allen. "The Deputy Sings." Columbia Records, 1960.

Case, Amanda. E-mail correspondence, via Facebook. December 13, 2009.

"The Crockett Craze," *Davy Crockett: The Complete Television Series*, Walt Disney Company, Buena Vista Home Entertainment, 2001.

Doug Abbott Collection

e/p partners TV

"Final Payment," aka "The Tycoon," written by Charles Marion. Robert B. Sinclair
    Teleplays Collection, PA Mss 12, Department of Special Collections, Univer-
    sity Libraries, University of California, Santa Barbara.

Garver, Kathy. E-mail correspondence. December 14, 2009.

"Hang the Law," written by Herbert Purdum. Robert B. Sinclair Teleplays Collec-
    tion, PA Mss 12, Department of Special Collections, University Libraries,
    University of California, Santa Barbara.

Lear, Norman. Personal interview. April 27, 2010.

"Marked for Bounty," written by William Yagermann. Robert B. Sinclair Tele-
    plays Collection, PA Mss 12, Department of Special Collections, University
    Libraries, University of California, Santa Barbara.

Marshall, Jack. "The Marshall Swings!" Capitol Records, 1960.

Morgan, Read. Personal interviews. January 18, 2010, and April 27, 2010.

"Parkinson," Henry Fonda interview program excerpts, accessed from "Young
    Mister Lincoln," DVD, The Criterion Collection. Program originally broad-
    cast on BBC- TV, November 1, 1975.

"Shadow of the Noose," written by Roland Kibbee. Robert B. Sinclair Teleplays
    Collection, PA Mss 12, Department of Special Collections, University Li-
    braries, University of California, Santa Barbara.

"The Two Faces of Bob Claxton," aka "The Kid," written by Charles O' Neal.
    Robert B. Sinclair Teleplays Collection, PA Mss 12, Department of Special
    Collections, University Libraries, University of California, Santa Barbara.

"TV's Western Heroes," Good Times Home Video Corporation, 1993.

"Presentation to Writers for a New Television Series—Tentatively Called The
    Deputy." Robert B. Sinclair Teleplays Collection, PA Mss 12, Department
    of Special Collections, University Libraries, University of California, Santa
    Barbara.

Personal Name Index
Covering chapters 1- 6

About the Author

Glenn A. Mosley is the Director of Broadcasting in the School of Journalism and Mass Media at the University of Idaho in Moscow, Idaho. A Massachusetts native, Glenn received his AA degree from Dean College in Franklin, MA, and his BA and MA degrees from the University of Maryland in College Park, MD. Most of his professional career has been spent as a news reporter and faculty member.

CPSIA information can be obtained
at www.ICGtesting.com
Printed in the USA
FFOW04n1649081115
18333FF